YOU NEED MORE MONEY

YOU NEED MORE MONEY

WAKE UP AND SOLVE YOUR
FINANCIAL PROBLEMS ONCE AND FOR ALL

Matt Manero

PORTFOLIO/PENGUIN

Portfolio/Penguin
An imprint of Penguin Random House LLC
375 Hudson Street
New York, New York 10014

Most Portfolio books are available at a discount when purchased in quantity for sales promotions or corporate use. Special editions, which include personalized covers, excerpts, and corporate imprints, can be created when purchased in large quantities. For more information, please call (212) 572-2232 or e-mail specialmarkets@penguinrandomhouse.com. Your local bookstore can also assist with discounted bulk purchases using the Penguin Random House corporate Business-to-Business program. For assistance in locating a participating retailer, e-mail B2B@penguinrandomhouse.com.

Library of Congress Cataloging-in-Publication Data

Names: Manero, Matt, author.
Title: You need more money : wake up and solve your financial problems
    once and for all / Matt Manero.
Description: New York : Portfolio, 2018.
Identifiers: LCCN 2018001908| ISBN 9780735216983 (hardback) |
    ISBN 9780735216990 (epub)
Subjects: LCSH: Finance, Personal. | BISAC: BUSINESS & ECONOMICS /
    Personal Finance / General. | SELF-HELP / Motivational & Inspirational.
Classification: LCC HG179 .M26327 2018 | DDC 332.024—dc23 LC record
    available at https://lccn.loc.gov/2018001908

Printed in the United States of America
10 9 8 7 6 5 4 3 2 1

Book design by Daniel Lagin

This book is dedicated to my family:

*my beloved wife, Rokki, and our three incredible boys,
John, Jack, and Julian.*

You are the reason I do everything I do.

RIP John B. Eibort

CONTENTS

CONTENTS

PART II
THE ROAD MAP

YOU NEED MORE MONEY

Introduction

Hello. I'm glad you're here. Something motivated you to pick up and open a book called *You Need More Money*. Maybe the title connected with you instantly, and you thought, *I do need more money. It's been on my mind for a long time. Enough messing around. Maybe this book will finally show me what to do about it.*

Or maybe it's a thought you never had before, and some mixture of curiosity and fear made you look. *Do I really need more money? Sure, I'd like to have more money, but do I really need it? Could this book tell me something I don't know about my finances?*

Or—and let's be real—maybe you picked up this book just to scoff at the title. *You Need More Money? Who is this Matt Manero guy and why does he think he can tell me how much money I need?*

If you're the first kind of reader, congratulations—you've

taken the first step toward drastically improving your financial situation: acknowledging that you need more money. And you've taken the second step, too: finding the book that will give you a clear road map to getting there. If you're the second kind of reader, let me end your curiosity and fear right now: You do need more money—a lot more than you think—and this book is going to show you exactly how to get it. If you follow the steps here, it's going to be a lot easier than you think. To the third kind of reader, I have to say: Sorry for the rude wake-up call, buddy, but no matter how much you think you've got, it's nowhere near enough, and however comfortable you think you are, I'll bet you aren't living the life you always dreamed of. I'm going to show you just how far short you are and what you're going to have to do to cover the gap.

No matter who you are, when it comes to your finances, chances are you thought you'd be further along by now. You'd be able to kick back more and worry about the future less. Well, it didn't happen. You're way behind, even more than you know, and you're too scared to face the truth. I'm betting you haven't discussed the state of your finances with your spouse, your children, your parents, or your brothers and sisters. Even the thought of that discussion gives you too much anxiety. And if you've said anything to your friends and neighbors, you sure as hell haven't told them the truth. Maybe they think you are doing great, killin' it even, and you take false comfort in maintaining their illusion. But you know that in reality you haven't put away enough for much of anything other than keeping up with the Joneses and perpetuating the lie: the lie that you are financially secure. But whether you're aware of it or choosing to ignore the reality, the truth is that everywhere you turn, your life is calling for more money. Money for bills, cars, lessons, tutors, the mortgage, eating out, vacations, college, retirement . . . the list goes on. It doesn't matter where the money comes from, you just need more of it. If that doesn't scare the hell out of you, it should. How, where, when are you going to catch up? Once you realize that *you need more money,* this is the question that keeps you up at night.

I know because it used to keep me up at night, too.

But I dug myself out. Not only did I climb out of the hopelessness, but I'm on top now. I'm forty-eight years old and I've been in business for myself since I was twenty-five. I started at the bottom of the barrel in business: no money, no contacts, no plan. I fought and clawed my way to eventually build a successful company from the ground up. Now I operate as president and CEO of three companies that produce annual business of over $100 million; but you won't see me slowing down, I still need MORE MONEY. Not to pay the bills anymore, but to fulfill my potential. To live my life to the fullest. To provide long-lasting security for my wife and our three boys. And to help more people.

The truth is, your picture of success probably isn't adequate. Whether you like it or not, we now live in a winner-take-all world. Working people haven't gotten a decent raise in decades, and the middle class is dying off. You need to climb into the ranks of the rich quickly, or risk being left behind. It's not enough to just stay on top of paying your bills; you also need to move the needle of your finances enough to create *real* wealth that can provide for you and your family into retirement and beyond. That's right. I want you to leave a ton of money for your heirs. Why would you want to leave them with nothing when you die? And even if you don't have heirs, you can leave behind a legacy and change the world by giving your fortune to a cause that matters to you. I want to generate so much money that it can last for generations. And I want the same for you and your family.

You better believe you can do it, too. I know you can, because I'm going to show you exactly how.

Maybe you think you messed up somewhere along the way, so you just gave up on the dreams you had earlier in your life. When you graduated, you said you would be a millionaire by the time you were thirty. Well, thirty came and went and instead of becoming a millionaire, you actually fell financially behind—way behind. You might actually be falling into the trap that millions of Americans fall into when they start to think that financial freedom is no longer attainable . . . they simply give up. They toss in the towel and say, *Not in my lifetime.*

This book will convince you that you have the potential—you just haven't tapped into it. You've tended to play it safe and you've lowered your goals because part of you is scared of shooting for something big. Perhaps you limped into your career or business, stayed small, played it safe, and made a decent living for yourself and your family. But you know you can do so much more. I know you can make *more* money. Maybe you just didn't know how . . . until now.

Let me make one thing clear—this is not a book that's going to show you how to make a little extra money on the side, how to get slightly better returns on your investments, or how to make incremental upgrades to your lifestyle. The methods I outline here are going to unleash your potential to earn and dramatically change your life. You're no longer going to plan your life around the money you have coming in. Instead, you're going to dream big, picture a lifestyle of your design, and take a giant leap into the kind of wealth you've only ever dreamed about.

Something is missing in most of us these days: *unbridled ambition*. A burning, unyielding desire to cross whatever finish line you desire. To stop playing it safe. You need to have so much ambition that the obstacles you face shrink in front of you. The utter *lack* of ambition is creating generations of people who settle for less. The odds are this is now you. You just don't want success badly enough. I'm talking about all areas of your life: success in relationships, success in careers, success in health, and, you better believe it, success in your bank account. What you really want is comfort, and comfort isn't going to get you where you want to go.

Together, we are going to build a "Lifestyle by Design." A life that you were meant for. For me, when it comes to success, I know that money is part of the equation, and I'm going to show you why it needs to be for you, too. I need you to understand that money plays a big role in happiness. Stop believing that crap that "money won't make you happy." It is simply not true.

Money matters, and it matters more than you have given it

credit for. You need more money to help you achieve your dreams and to give you peace of mind. To give you freedom. Whether you want to make a change to your own life or to the world around you, money gives you the power and courage to put your vision into action.

Money is not the pursuit of greed. It is not something to be ashamed of or boastful about. Rather, money is like oxygen. In my mind, it is a requirement of happiness—because money helps you live a Lifestyle by Design . . . *your* design. Regardless of whether you want to have the private jet, the mansions, the trips to exotic locations, or maybe just an early retirement so you can spend your life golfing all day, you can't do any of it to the fullest without a constant stream of income. *You Need More Money* provides you the *freedom* and security so that when you are doing what you were meant to do, you can do it to the fullest.

Lastly, you will need a guide to take you through it all. While you need more money than you think, and though you have further to go than you think, getting there is not as complicated as you might imagine. The journey from where you are (even if you're broke) to getting rich enough to live the life you've always wanted can be broken down into six simple steps. And I'm going to break down each one of those steps for you in ways that apply to you and your situation.

But first, you're going to need a wake-up call.

This book is divided into two parts. In *Part I: The Wake-up Call*, it is time to *wake the hell up*. I'm going to shake you out of what I call the "False Positive," the illusion that you're doing all right, which can be shattered at any moment. Life comes at you fast in ways you can't expect. We'll take a hard look at why the only way to be prepared is to have more money. Once you've woken up to the reality that YOU NEED MORE MONEY, I'm going to show you how changing your money mind-set—the way you think and talk about money—is the most fundamental thing holding you back. You're going to go from being a "Blamer" to being a "Game Facer." While those around you waste their time and money trying to keep up with each other, you'll be quietly zooming past them as you stack and rack cash to put toward achieving your ultimate ambitions.

In *Part II: The Road Map*, I'll give you the tangible, step-by-step process to make it happen. We're going to evaluate the gap between your current financial state and how much money you need to live your Lifestyle by Design, then chart a course to launching yourself into real wealth. We're going to find the right people to help you on your journey, and immediately start putting aside money to invest in your dreams. We'll identify your superpower—the skill or quality you can rely on as you build your wealth—and evaluate whether you can ascend to great heights in your current organization, or whether you need to switch jobs, switch industries, or even go out on your own and build a "Personal ATM" to close your money gap.

Income stagnation and the lack of real savings are epidemics in the United States of America. But you can do better: change your financial future and break the chain of habits instilled in you by your parents, your siblings, and your friends. Today is the day that you and I start to make it happen. I am your advocate, I am your coach, and I am your confidant, but most important, I am your biggest fan. I want you to win. But it's *you* who will need to put the strategies into action. I started from the absolute bottom and worked my way up to financial security, all without a mentor or much knowledge. If I can do that, then not only can you do it, but you have an advantage because you now have the benefit of everything I've learned to catapult you into success. Not only can you win at this, but *I want you to beat me*. Nothing would make me happier than to get a call or an e-mail from you telling me how you kicked the shit out of my money. That would be the greatest gift of all: to have helped you beat me at my own game. But know this: I'm ridiculously competitive. And you'll need to be the same way if you want more. More love, more achievements, more success, and, damn straight, more money. Let the games begin, my friend . . .

PART I
THE WAKE-UP CALL

CHAPTER 1

Your Money Mind-set Is Broken

IT CAN ALL CHANGE IN AN INSTANT

When my brother-in-law, John, moved from Little Rock, Arkansas, to Dallas, Texas, with his wife and four children a few years ago, my family was thrilled. It allowed us all, my family of five, his family of six, and my mother-in-law—Gigi—to see each other a lot. Our favorite tradition was Easter Sunday at Gigi's house. She cooked, the children played football outside together, and Gigi and my beloved wife, Rokki, were able to dote on John. John and Rokki are technically half brother and sister, but if you ever mentioned that, they would both kick your ass. To say that Rokki, her sister, Jennell, and Gigi were crazy in love with John would be an understatement. They were fiercely protective of him and worshipped the ground he walked on.

You see, life was always a little difficult for John. His birth father never made an impact in his life and his adoptive father was worthless. Gigi's first husband, the father of John and his sister, Jennell, was nonexistent. After John was born, he was gone. When Gigi remarried, she and her new husband had Rokki. Rokki's dad left the family when she was eleven and no one heard from him for three full years. After that divorce, Gigi remarried again to a "real winner," who basically showed them the world of drinking, laziness, and negativity. My wife got away from it all at sixteen, when she moved in with her best friend to finish high school with some structure, but the impact of an absent father left John without a road map.

John did the best he could without any guidance. High school was a challenge, he never considered college, and he went into the workforce underskilled. But through it all—his mother's husbands, the lack of father figures, and any authority figures leaving their family—John was always there for the women in his life. Rokki, Jennell, and Gigi considered that enough to earn 110 percent of their love, and they made sure John knew it every chance they could. In their eyes, he could do no wrong. And once again, if my wife, her sister, or her mom heard you criticize John, they would drop gloves and fight you on the spot. See, John's financial situation was like chicken and feathers: At times he was eating chicken, and at other times he was eating feathers. It was always an up-and-down situation, fueled by household moves, job changes, and the idea that the "next" job would be the home run.

On Easter Sunday in 2014, when John and his family came

to the door at Gigi's, we all jumped up and shared hugs. The kids ran outside and it had all the makings of another great Easter at Gigi's house. But when I got to John, he looked exhausted. His skin was pale and, without question, he had dropped weight.

I hugged him and said, "Wow, John, you have lost some weight!"

"Maybe five pounds," said John.

More like twenty to twenty-five pounds, I thought.

When dinner was served, I noticed that John hardly touched his plate. Gigi always made a ton of food because of how much John and I would gulp down, but today he hardly ate a bite. It was odd, but we didn't comment much on it. After dinner, John and I hit the couch to watch the game. Within minutes John was asleep. I sat by his side, watching the game quietly. Around fifteen minutes later, John awoke suddenly, almost in a panic. His eyes shot wide open as he grabbed my arm and leaned over to me. He said in a whisper, "I haven't felt worth a shit in months, but I'm going to the doctor in the morning to get it checked out."

That should have been that. My brother-in-law, loved by so many, especially his wife and four children, and considered superhuman by my wife, his sister, and his mother, should have simply gone to the doctor on Monday, gotten a shot, and gone back to work on Tuesday. But John wasn't okay. The doctor he saw on Monday sent him straight to the emergency room. At age forty-six, and—as we were soon to find out—with no health insurance, no life insurance, and less than $100 in the bank, our beloved John was diagnosed with stage 4 cancer. Our lives, none of them, would ever be the same again.

THE DIFFERENCE MONEY CAN MAKE

Normal can change in an instant. Firings, regulations, buyouts, mergers, or even a cancer diagnosis can occur without any of it being your fault. My brother-in-law had busted his butt for twenty years, had nothing to show for it, and was filled with guilt when he discovered he was dying. For years, he'd known that he needed more money to keep his family secure, but now it was too late.

At this point in my life, I already had the wake-up call that made me realize I needed more money. My brother-in-law's stage 4 cancer only convinced me that I could never rest. I didn't stop when I was doing okay because I knew it all could change in a minute—and it did. While this kind of tragedy showed me how a lack of money and preparation can cause havoc, on the other side, I saw the power that having money can make on a difficult situation. The outpouring of emotional support from the community of Coppell, Texas, was incredible: people provided food, gifts, clothes, and even some cash. But when it came to ultimately helping with the money situation, whether it was John's past-due bills or the rent, Rokki and I were able to step in and take care of it so John's family could hold things together during his sickness. Being able to write checks without worrying about how it would affect my family's future is the greatest gift I have ever been fortunate enough to give.

Finding yourself in a situation like John's would be devastating, but even less extreme circumstances can cause a major crisis. You want to be in the spot where you don't have to worry about what would happen if everything in your life changed. Right now, you don't have enough savings, enough wealth, and enough of a plan, and it's finally time to admit it: *you need more money.* Acknowledging that is the first step to changing your financial situation, and your life. If everything goes south tomorrow, you're screwed. You don't have enough money saved, the college account for your children is underfunded, as is your retirement account, and if just one little blip hits your financial situation, it's all going to come tumbling down. Would you be okay if everything changed? I doubt it. And it should keep you up at night, just like it did for me.

I tell you this to make you understand two things. First, understand how quickly your financial situation can change. The vast majority of things in this world are out of your control. You can't control how new regulations will affect your business, the strength of new competitors, how returns on the stock market will pay out, or even what health issues may arise. All of this means you need to focus harder on the one thing you can control: you need to get your money in order.

Second, you need to understand the power that money gives you. I'm not talking about power for the sake of prestige or notoriety or fame. I'm talking about the power to lift the guilt from a dying man's shoulders. When I saw that my brother-in-law was scared of dying and leaving his family with nothing because he hadn't gotten his finances into shape, my wife and I were able to step in because of our financial success and remove the burden from his shoulders so he could focus on his recovery.

Chances are you'll face a time in your life when a family member or close friend faces a crisis and needs all the help they can get. It may not even be that they need help paying the bills—if you have a sick friend, they may just want you to be by their side. Can you afford to take time off work to spend time with them? Can you afford to let your friend's wife borrow your car to do errands? Can you pay to get their air conditioner or heater fixed? Good news can cause a crisis, too. Maybe your insanely smart niece gets into an Ivy League school, but your sister can't afford the tuition. Aren't you going to want to pitch in? In these kinds of situations, too many people find themselves unable to offer much of a helping hand, since they are too busy struggling with their own financial worries. When you're rich, you'll find that you have a lot more freedom and flexibility to drop everything in a crisis so you can focus on the thing that really matters, without having to worry about missing a paycheck.

FALSE POSITIVE: WHEN YOU THINK YOU'RE DOING OKAY—BUT REALLY, YOU'RE BROKE

Until my brother-in-law's diagnosis, I thought he had been doing okay financially. You probably think you're doing okay, too. You might be at the point where you are able to pay the bills and take your significant other out for a nice steak dinner. Hell, you might actually be able to go on nice vacations and drive nice cars. But that is the problem: You are spending your future income today at an alarming rate. You are living in what I call False Positive.

False Positive is believing that you are doing better than you actually are. Just because you can purchase something without overdrawing your bank account *doesn't mean you can afford it.* The biggest, and most detrimental, lie you can tell yourself is "I'm okay financially." Once you start to believe that you are okay financially, you'll start to get irresponsible with your money—and that doesn't just mean spending more than you should. You'll also take your hand off the throttle and stop pushing yourself to increase your earnings.

I see it all the time in my business of equipment financing. My company finances heavy equipment like big rigs and heavy-duty tow trucks. I hear customers tell me all the time, "My trucks are paid for . . . I'm in good shape." And you know what they do? They don't charge enough for their services; therefore, they don't have enough cash left over for long-term repair and maintenance, and they end up falling behind and never catch up. The lack of pressure because of no payments due or any debt service allows the financial grim reaper—complacency—to creep in. While they think they are in a position of strength, a competitor who is 100 percent on his game suddenly shows up on their territory and eats their lunch. The same thing can happen to you in your personal financial journey. If you fall into False Positive and stop pushing for more income, more savings, more stacks and racks of cash, you, too, can get complacent and eventually be caught off guard.

Today is the day you stop living in False Positive. False Positive is the single most dangerous deterrent to financial success. It tricks you into believing that you aren't broke just because you're able to make ends meet. **You need to realize that even when you're paying your bills on time and have a little extra left over in the bank, the moment you factor in future expenses of retirement, child care, and health care, your financial picture starts to look grim. Most people think that being broke is only for the lowest earners, but many people who earn good money are actually broke, too.** Here's a simple rule of thumb to figure out whether you're broke: You're broke if you *have* to go to work each day to earn a paycheck to pay your bills this week, and you don't have much of a choice about it. Broke is being unable to quit your dead-end job to free yourself up to look for a better one because you can't afford to go two to three months without a paycheck. Broke is a terrible place to live. There's no freedom and certainly no wiggle room in the event of a crisis. If you haven't taken a long, hard look at how close you are to being broke, you're not just lying to others about how well you're doing . . . you're lying to yourself. You will look for *any* evidence that you are doing better than you think: closing a small deal, or getting a 3 percent yearly raise, even getting a tax refund check (which is really your own money you've let Uncle Sam hold for a year). But these little bumps don't create wealth. They are just helping you live in False Positive, making you think that you're doing okay. The False Positive test at the end of this chapter will help you determine whether you're really doing okay or just fooling yourself.

THE NUMBERS YOU'RE AIMING FOR ARE TOO LOW

Part of what keeps many people in False Positive is a warped sense of what counts as good money today.

$100K Ain't What It Used to Be

When I graduated from college in 1991, in order to be considered in the top 1 percent of all earners in America, you needed to earn $100,000 per year. Today, in order to be in the top 1 percent of all earners you need to earn $384,000 per year. You can see instantly how $100,000 doesn't stretch how it used to. Yet so many people still think that $100,000 is a lot of money. And look, if you don't earn anywhere close to that, then, yes, $100,000 is a lot of money to you. But just because you don't earn it doesn't mean it's good. It's fine to chase a number, as long as it's accurate, but, when it comes to money, most of us are still chasing numbers that have long passed their level of meaningfulness.

Let me show you exactly what I mean by simply comparing the cost of basic living expenses from 2000 versus 2014. You will quickly see that it simply takes more money to live.

	2000	2014
Average home price	$161,000	$242,000
Average monthly rent	$635	$890
New car	$20,300	$31,500
Movie ticket	$5.25	$10.25
Gas (per gallon)	$1.27	$3.51
Annual health care	$4,550	$9,300

Basically, the cost of living has increased 31 percent between 2000 and 2014. But the earning power of most Americans has not kept up. During this time, the wages of the lowest percentile of wage earners has actually *decreased* by 3 percent and the highest bracket of earners has only increased 9 percent. What that means is that the lowest income bracket actually *lost* income and buying power. Therefore, regardless of whether you are at the top or the bottom of the earning scale, your wage increase has not kept up with the increase in living expenses. Without a doubt, the money has moved. Have you moved with it?

Being a Millionaire Isn't Good Enough Either

All right, you might be thinking, if an annual income of $100,000 isn't good enough, maybe I should be dreaming of becoming a millionaire. So many of us are still chasing the millionaire dream. It just sounds so nice: "I'm a Millionaire."

There is only one problem. If you can get any millionaire to open up about it, they'll tell you it's not as much as you think it is. Becoming a millionaire was a worthy goal in the 1950s, '60s, and maybe the '70s, but since those decades, it just isn't what it once was. As I've just shown you, a dollar doesn't stretch like it used to. And while being a millionaire is nice, it certainly doesn't have the same impact as it did even as little as a decade ago. Remember, the money has moved.

What's more, it's still moving. If a dollar doesn't stretch now as far as it used to, it's going to stretch even less by the time you hit retirement.

I say all this to make one point: **you need more than $1 million when you retire.**

Let's look at a million-dollar retirement investment. If you have $1 million saved up by retirement and you put it in a conservative investment of tax-free municipal bonds that pay a 3 percent annual rate of return, your million will pay you $30,000 a year, or $2,500 a month. Add to it the average Social Security benefit (if it doesn't run out . . .) of $1,366 a month, and your "millionaire status" affords you a lifestyle of $3,866 a month. And let's not forget that $3,866 in the future will not stretch as much as it does today. It's not exactly going to pay for Tuscany in the summer, a first-class flight to Bali, or any of the other fantasies you imagined in your golden years as a millionaire. And helping your son or daughter pay for your grandchildren's education? Forget about it. *Your kids* are going to be paying for you to come visit them.

Let's say you wanted to live on $100,000 per year in retirement. Your tax-free municipal bond investment and your entire nest egg would be gone in approximately eleven years. The average American life expectancy of a man is pushing eighty years old, and a woman pushing slightly higher than eighty years old. Therefore, if you retired at sixty-five years old, you would be broke by seventy-six and still have four (or more) years to live.

Once again, while a million dollars is substantially more than the average American has saved in their life, it's not nearly as much as you think. I need you to get this point. Don't compare yourself to the average American because the average American struggles to make ends meet in retirement. The purpose of this book is to open up your eyes, reignite your fuel, to squash your complacency, and to give you the road map to not just 1 million dollars, but *millions* of dollars to live the life and achieve the dreams that most of us actually have.

ACTION STEP: THE FALSE POSITIVE TEST

Think you're above all this? Then take my False Positive test and we'll see:

How many of the statements below are true of your current financial situation?

1. You have at least six months of savings—not 401(k), not retirement, but cash sitting in the bank. If you lost your job today, your savings would cover you for all your expenses for six months.
2. You have a credit rating of 700 or above.
3. You are paying your bills from current cash and not from debt.
4. For every decade starting with age twenty, you have:
   - Age 20–29—you have 1X (one full year of) your annual income or more as your net worth. Net worth is simply your assets (what you own) minus your liabilities (what you owe).
   - Age 30–39—you have 3X (three full years of) your annual income or more as your net worth.
   - Age 40–49—you have 5X (five full years of) your annual income or more as your net worth.
   - Age 50 and above—you have 10X (ten full years of) your annual income or more as your net worth.

If you have fewer than three of the four ... WARNING: FALSE POSITIVE ALERT. You're playing with fire, and it could all change in an instant. If you're confused about how well you're really doing, let me break the news for you: **You are broke** and you need to fix that immediately. Over the next few chapters, I'm going to show you exactly how.

If you have items one, two, and three covered, congratulations, you're better off than most people. You have the flexibility to quit and look for a higher-paying job, or cushion yourself from a minor crisis like a fender bender. But you *still* need more money if you want to have any hope of doing the things you've dreamed of, whether it's retiring at forty-five or paying for your kids to go to a private academy. But you're not really out of False Positive until you satisfy the conditions of item four. This formula works as an incredible baseline for you to base your financial health against. Let me explain why:

The Key Formula—1X, 3X, 5X, 10X

I've tested this formula against hundreds of people. I have tested it against the poorest and the wealthiest people I know, and we all agree it works and is accurate. The reason this formula works so well is that it forces both low earners and high earners to check their spending. I know people who earn $250,000 per year, who are in their fifties, and have less than 1X their annual income as their net worth. This is why most Americans are actually broke. They spend it all.

If you are twenty-five years old and earn $50,000 per year in income, you should have a net worth of $50,000. This means that you should have assets (what you own) minus liabilities (what you owe) that equal $50,000.

As your income and age increase, so does the demand for a more robust net worth. **In the final stage of my formula, you will be in your fifties and you should have a net worth of 10X your annual income. Thus, if you are earning $250,000 per** year at that time, you should have a net worth of $2,500,000. Do this math now, and determine your own result.

Odds are, you are behind—way behind. In some cases, you're still broke, so you're going to need to keep reading. But trust me, I'm going to help you get ahead of the curve to get out of broke faster—which is good for you!

CHAPTER 2

Fixing Your Money Mind-set

PANIC MODE

Rokki called me in a panic on that Tuesday to tell me my brother-in-law John was admitted to the emergency room and of his diagnosis. John had advanced germ cell cancer. This is a type of cancer normally reserved for young boys, with a high cure rate. Unfortunately, adults with germ cell have a much lower cure rate. The cancer gets into their lungs, and, according to the editorial board at www.cancer.net, while children have a survival rate of 87 percent, it is much, much lower in adults. If you've ever received news like this, you know the strength of the gut punch it delivers. It takes your breath away in an instant. Every emotion in your body fires up on the spot and it is a miracle you can stand up straight. For my wife and Gigi, they couldn't. When I arrived home they were sobbing uncontrollably. How could this happen to John? He was the only man in their lives, other than me, who had never left them.

As a businessman, I went into fix-it mode. We put a plan together, and getting John better was our mission. We questioned the doctors, Googled everything, and pulled together to beat this thing. Within a day, Rokki and I had what was like a task force assembled between our family, John's family, and Jennell, and Gigi, and we were going to be a force to be reckoned with. I went to see John to talk about the money. Don't fool yourself—there is no zero-down financing with cancer. You need to have insurance and some real cash working for you to get the best treatment. I told him that together we were going to kick cancer and he was going to be okay.

"Let me help you," I said. "You focus on getting better and I will handle the financial details. Let's talk about how we can work with your insurance provider to get you the best care. Who is your insurance provider?"

John looked at me. "I don't have insurance," he responded.

"No insurance?" I said.

"None," said John.

"Okay," I said. "How about cash? How much do you and Lori have?"

"Less than a hundred bucks," he said.

"No health insurance and less than a hundred dollars in the bank?" I replied. I was puzzled. "I don't understand. You've worked for more than twenty-five years. Some years were lean, but some were good years for you. I thought you had a 401(k) when you worked for the BMW dealer?"

"I did, but I cashed it in a few years ago." He paused and looked away. "Matt, there's more. I'm ten months behind on the rent on the house."

As nuts as it sounds, John was actually ten months behind on his rent and, charmer that he was, kept talking his landlord into letting him stay.

John took a deep breath. "I don't have life insurance either. If we don't kick this . . . my family will have nothing. Zero. Not a dime."

I kept a stern face for John, but inside, I was in shock. My mind was racing on this news. How could this have happened? After more than twenty-five years of work, John literally had no life insurance, no health insurance, a rented house, and less than $100 in the bank. I had had a sense that John was behind financially, but I never could have imagined such a dire situation.

John had always been handsome, a sharp dresser, and good with small talk, which made everyone like him instantly—especially me. We had known each other for nineteen years and during that time, we never had a cross word. But the one thing he never liked to discuss was money. When he was between jobs, I often tried to bring up the question of finances, but John always shut down the conversation by saying, "I have time. I know I'm behind, but I have time." John had worked for me twice, and despite how difficult it can be to work with family, for us it was fine. I always wanted to help John move to the next level financially, especially because Rokki wanted her brother to be elevated past broke. But our time in the office together didn't create the results any of us wanted. When we parted ways, both times, it never created issues between us. John always knew that I would love and cherish his baby sister, and I'm sure that had a lot to do with our friendship.

John and I talked often about what his true calling or his superpower might be, and we realized it was in the church. John was powerful and accepted in the church. He was himself there, and he could have been an amazing youth pastor, or maybe even pastor of a church. But instead, because he always was behind with money, he spent most of his career as a salesperson, struggling to get out from under his debts. The pressure of constantly borrowing from Peter to pay Paul steals freedom from millions and millions of people, and it stole from my brother-in-law John. It stole opportunity, happiness, a good night's sleep, quality time with his kids, and his freedom to live his Lifestyle by Design. In the end, cancer and the stress of chasing money stole his life.

Why was John so secretive about his finances? Why are any of us so secretive? How did the discussion of money become so private and guarded? Maybe it's because we feel ashamed when we're not doing well and embarrassed when we are. When we're not doing well, we think it says something about our character and who we are at our core. We know we could—and should—be doing better, so we don't want to let people know where we are lest we be judged. When we are doing well, we're nervous that people will judge us as boastful or moneygrubbing. The first step to fixing your money mind-set is to let go of these anxieties and accept the truth of your financial situation. Get honest with it all now, with yourself and with the people who matter to you. Don't wait until it is too late to get real with your money situation. If you don't face the truth voluntarily, you'll eventually be forced to face it.

"Matt," John said to me, "I can't earn money now. Please do me a favor: don't let my family go homeless."

When you look into the eyes of a friend or family member who has been diagnosed with stage 4 cancer, you see right through to his heart. There is no disguising that he might die. The truth jumps out at you like a fire that just got a dose of lighter fluid. I saw firsthand how the guilt of not being prepared in a life-and-death situation creates the ultimate vulnerability. As I looked at John, after these revelations, I had only one answer for him, the answer that Rokki and I would both easily come to agree upon.

"There isn't a snowball's chance in hell that Rokki or I would ever let that happen," I assured him. "I promise you. We will handle the money situation for you. We got you, John. Rokki and I got you covered. You just focus on getting better."

I hugged him and left to get to work.

HOW I LEARNED TO BE HONEST ABOUT MONEY

For many of my years in business, I was broke or nearly broke, and I couldn't be honest about it, not even with my own wife.

In the early days of our marriage, on Friday nights, when I

got home after a long week of busting my ass, Rokki would ask me, "How did we do this week?"

Most Friday nights I would lie to her and tell her we did well. She would smile and leave it alone . . . until the cracks in my lies started to show. Like when our electric got cut off and we couldn't pay the full balance.

I made up a convoluted explanation for why we were behind on our bills. I was too much of a wimp to tell her the simple truth: that we didn't have the money to pay the bill in full. I ended up having to borrow money just to make the minimum payment to get the lights turned back on.

This game went on for too long in our marriage. Not for days, weeks, or months, but *years*. Years of hiding behind a struggling business that could barely pay my household bills, let alone fund savings, retirement, or college accounts. Most Fridays I would lie and tell my wife business was good, and as long as the lights were turned on, she would leave it alone.

Gradually, though, Rokki started to see through my BS. When business started to take such a bad turn that I couldn't even borrow money to make up the shortfall, it became impossible to hide it, and Rokki stopped being nice about it.

I slowly realized that I couldn't keep up this pattern of lies, and had to come clean. I remember the one Friday night when I decided to finally tell Rokki the truth, without making excuses or trying to sugarcoat it. I came clean about everything . . . that I hadn't been telling her the truth about the real state of our finances. That we were actually struggling and not doing as well as I had led her to believe.

Rokki asked me if I paid myself for the week, and I said, "No."

She looked at me with disgust. "How could you do that to us? How could you do that to me and our boys?" Then she said, "I'm going to ask you one more question, did you pay your employees?"

I said, "Yes."

When I told her this, she lost her mind. She started stamping her feet and crying uncontrollably.

"What is the matter with you? Why would you choose your employees over us? One day, Matt, you will realize you are so much bigger than your business."

Then she ran into our bedroom and slammed the door, leaving me in silence. I spent the night on the couch, unable to sleep. I was used to disappointing myself for years, but my wife? My boys? My family? Disappointing her was the ultimate low. She didn't care about the money. Hell, when we married I had nothing, so love was all we had. But she sure as hell didn't like being lied to. Coming clean and facing Rokki's anger and disappointment were the catalysts I needed to change. That night, I resolved to do two things: (1) build a $100 million business, and (2) make sure my wife never worried about our money situation again.

Today, I can proudly say that I've done both. My first company, Commercial Fleet Financing, Inc., has now funded over $1 billion in equipment loans and leases. We are one of the largest independent finance companies In the equipment financing industry. After I made that commitment on the couch that night, it took me only eighteen months to reach the $100-million-per-year goal I set on that Friday night on the couch, and my sweet Rokki never asked me about our money situation again. Just eighteen months later, I wasn't just out of the poorhouse—I had rocketed out of the middle class forever.

GETTING HONEST IS THE KEY

How did I turn my business around in such a short time, when I had struggled for years just to keep it afloat? It all changed that night I decided to come clean. The relief I felt at telling Rokki the truth was incredible. I no longer felt that suffocating guilt that had been driving a wedge between us. You know that feeling, don't you? The lack of self-worth, the shame that the lie causes you to feel. Facing the facts and putting on my big-boy pants to tell my wife the truth was liberating. When I stopped worrying about maintaining the appearance of doing okay, I was able to free myself to focus on fixing the business and get on track to not be average. I committed to altering the situation once and for all. I drew a line in the sand on that day, and that was all it took for me to blast off with 100 percent, unwavering commitment.

You have that same power. The power to draw a line in the sand today, right now, that will remove the guilt, clean the slate, and catapult you to financial freedom. Stop lying to

yourself and everyone else. **Commit to owning your current financial situation and stop the cover-up.**

I will walk with you side by side as you read this book, to provide you with the support and the real-life tactics that will set you free and allow you to put your money guilt behind you once and for all.

We constantly lie to ourselves and hide the truth about our finances from the people around us. But getting honest is the first step to breaking out of our fear of money and empowering ourselves to take control of it.

Money wants to be submissive. It wants you to tame it, to take full control of it, and manhandle it. But until you decide to do just that, it will boss and slap you around. It's time to move up the food chain, get out of Broke and the middle class, and move into Rich. And it all starts with recognizing and changing your money mind-set.

WHAT'S YOUR MONEY MIND-SET?

Many people do not earn the income they deserve or need because of the pressure their surroundings put on them regarding money. They have either grown up with, or bought into, a mindset based on their circumstances, and that determines how they feel, talk about, and act toward money.

The way I see it, you can sort people into three categories depending on the mind-set they currently have about money: the Blamers, the Dreamers, and the Game Facers.

Every broke person I know has the same mind-set about money, which is why I call them the "Blamers."

Besides the fact that a person with a Blamer mind-set will never admit the truth about their money, here's what you can expect to hear from a Blamer:

- "Money won't make you happy."
- "I'm not money-motivated."
- "Money is the root of all evil."
- "The economy is bad."
- "I didn't grow up with money . . ."

The Blamers are the ones who would much rather not have conversations about money and, when they do, are always full of excuses for why they're broke. They make these excuses because in reality, they think their financial situation is never their fault and they believe there's nothing they can do to change it. Blamers also find ways to trick themselves into thinking they have enough.

Meanwhile, every stuck-in-middle-class person I know has the same mind-set about money: I call them the "Dreamers." I know I'm talking to a Dreamer when I hear things like:

- "I need more money, but I don't know how to get it."
- "Someday . . . when I win the lottery."
- "When I become a millionaire . . ."
- "I'm doing okay and if I just work a little harder, I'll get there."

Dreamers want to make more money but they aren't *doing* anything to make those dreams a reality. They think that more money will just happen to them without understanding that they need to work smarter and get in gear to go and get it for themselves.

Finally, every rich person I know has the same mind-set about money, which garners them the label "Game Facers." They say things like:

- "I need more money, I've worked out a plan for how I'm going to get it, and I'm putting my plan into action."
- "Money solves problems."
- "Money is a tool that should be used to make more money."
- "Money provides me *freedom,* and freedom is the end goal."

Game Facers always have their game face on and want nothing more than to jump in and face the game when it comes to their financial situation. They don't mess around—they are ready to play offense when it comes to their finances, and they play the game of money to win.

I've observed these mind-sets in action on the second Tuesday of every month at a poker game that's been hosted by my old neighbor Stanley (you will hear more about him later) for the past thirteen years. The same group shows up every month, and most of them are about twenty-five years older than me. Whenever we're at Stanley's place, something fascinating happens when the topic of money comes up. My friend Stanley, arguably the most well-off member, is always happy to talk about money. Jack, who made a ton of money and saved a ton of it, almost feels guilty because of his money, but never shies away from getting into a discussion about it. Stanley and Jack are both clear Game Facers. Mike, who had money and lost it, wants us all to still think he has it—because he is a Dreamer, he isn't awake to the fact that he is broke. Bobby, who made a lot of money and has a wife who refuses to let him keep it because of their spending habits, has clouded his mind to think he has enough—another trait of classic Dreamers, who don't live in reality that they are not okay. And Charley, who never really made a lot of money, spent every last dime of it, and is the first to ask if he can take your plate to the kitchen when we talk about money (he literally leaves the room when we talk about money)—yup, he's a Blamer.

And then there's me: twenty-five years younger than these guys, and for most of the history of the game, I didn't have any real money (I was a Dreamer for way too long before I got it together and became a Game Facer). But even though there were moments during all that time when I felt ashamed by how broke I was, I never shied away from a conversation about money. I knew I wasn't going to learn anything or change if I didn't see talking about money as an opportunity. Instead, I perked my ears up, listened, and asked questions. When Stanley or Jack had something to say on the topic of money, I made sure to pay attention and understand what they were talking about and how they learned what they knew. These two guys had played the game right, had worked their way to real wealth, and I was lucky enough to be at a table with them. Every poker night was an opportunity for me to learn from them, and work through my money struggles so that they could tell it to me straight and help me reach my full potential.

BLAME NO ONE BUT YOURSELF

The Blamer mind-set is toxic to success. The first step to getting out of it is admitting that your money situation is your fault. It's not the fault of the people with the money, or the government, or your parents, or your employer. You either have enough money or you don't, and either way, you have no one to blame but yourself. It is not the government who kept you from paying your bills. It is not the billionaire fat cats on Wall Street who took your piece of the American pie. It's not because your parents didn't have enough money either. In the end, when all the BS you, your friends, and your deadbeat family members tell you is over, it is *you* who put you where you are.

The good news is, you're in control. By owning all of your financial missteps, you can start to take steps in the right direction. **It's all up to you—and only you. If you pull yourself out of Broke, you are the reason. If you started from nothing and have made it to the middle class, give yourself a quick pat on the back because you got yourself there. But don't for a second forget the message of this book: regardless of your current financial status, YOU NEED MORE MONEY, I NEED MORE MONEY, WE ALL NEED MORE MONEY!** There is no time to rest on your laurels—it's back to the grind until you have enough money to live the life that matches your wants, wishes, and needs—what I call the ability to lead your Lifestyle by Design— *your* design.

Now, a death or divorce *can* hurt you financially and may be out of your control. Divorce and death are both very real and rarely do they provide financial benefit, if not leave you completely financially unaffected. But even in the face of these difficulties, it is YOU who must pull yourself up by your bootstraps and fix it. You have to come to grips with the fact that—for better or for worse—you are in control of the situation. Your boss did not make you broke. Neither did the company you work for. In fact, both of them contributed to your success by paying you a check that is cashable at the end of every pay period. You and your employer made a deal when you started working: You would provide the company with effort and hopefully results, and they would provide you with a check that clears. Most companies will honor this agreement for a very long time.

What if you work for a company at which the check they provide you doesn't clear? Or you freelance, or have work on the side, and provide services to a client who doesn't pay on time? Well, once again, that is your fault for sticking around. I am amazed at how many people I interview who tell me that the reason they are leaving their current position is because their employer bounced their paycheck. When I push them for how long this has been going on, the answer is always weeks or months. It is *never* once. They stayed with the employer out of loyalty, fear, or stupidity. They told themselves it would be fine, and fell into False Positive. Every time I encounter one of these people and hear these excuses, I have to snap them out of it: you are the person that didn't have the balls to stop being taken advantage of and leave. I understand it is easier to blame "the man," but in order to get closer to having more money, you need to take full responsibility for your future *and* current money situation.

Drop the BS. No more excuses about who or what is keeping you down. When people are successful, others say and think things about them like, "Wow, they really made something of themselves!" or "They really worked hard for their success!" Well, just as you can take the credit for financial success, unfortunately, you have to take all the blame for failure, too. If you end up settling for a small life, it will be your fault. If you end up living a life filled with adventure, luxury, and no financial worries, you will be able to take all the credit. This choice is now yours to make.

YOU HAVE TO DREAM, BUT DON'T STAY A DREAMER

Too many people are stuck in the Dreamer mind-set. I know you're thinking: *Matt, how can I live the life of my dreams if I don't dream in the first place? Dreaming is how I know what to work for and where to go.* I get it. And you're right, you do. **In order to achieve greatness, you need to dream big and visualize**

the life you've always wanted. And hey, Dreamers are great at doing this, but they also get stuck dreaming, never really achieving progress toward their goals. It's all dreaming, no action. I'm sure you have a friend like this, the one who's always talking about how much money she's going to make when she quits her dead-end job and starts her own business, how clients will be lined up outside her door, and how she's going to use that new-found wealth to travel the world . . . except none of it ever materializes. Your friend keeps working the same dead-end job, promising that she's going to quit when the time is right. This kind of dreaming is never going to take you anywhere and it's the kind that paralyzes your financial situation. In the next chapter I'm going to show you a structured way to dream your ideal life, and then give you the concrete steps you need to turn that from a dream into reality.

GAME FACERS HAVE SELF-ESTEEM AND ASK THE RIGHT QUESTIONS

The one thing all Blamers and Dreamers have in common is a lack of self-esteem. Before you can start to close your money gap, you've got to remove all the obstacles keeping you from your financial goal line. It's going to take guts to make the millions of dollars you need to get you and your family into a position that allows you to lead your Lifestyle by Design. In order to have the guts to start the course, stay the course, and finish the course, you will need to fix your self-esteem.

Self-esteem matters because you need the confidence to act and really push yourself in your race to make more money. In order to execute your plan and take action on it, you must have clarity on this. You can't spend your time thinking, *Am I worthy? Do I have what it takes? What can I give the person who already has everything? Do my partners respect me? Can I bring anything to their table? Am I successful enough to talk to him?*

Game Facers don't ask these kinds of questions. The kinds of questions we ask ourselves determine how healthy our self-esteem is. Asking questions that make you doubt yourself undermines your self-esteem and sucks the energy you need to move the needle of your net worth. Do both of us a favor and drop it now. You do need to honestly evaluate yourself and your abilities—that's where doubt has its place. But while Blamers and Dreamers ask self-defeating questions, Game Facers ask questions that enable them to get ahead, like, "What is the best use of my time in service of my goals?" or "What skills should I be developing so I can jump ahead in my career?" In order to *be* worthy of achieving your dreams, you must *believe* that you are worthy of achieving your dreams. Training yourself to have high self-esteem will make all the difference in your thought and action process.

Blamers and Game Facers answer the same questions differently. Let's take some examples of questions you might ask yourself when it comes to business, and the differences between how you might have answered yourself before and how I want you to answer yourself now to get rid of the excuses:

Question #1: Is now the time for me to ask for a raise?

Blamer's answer: My boss hates me. She never gives raises, so why even try?

Game Facer's answer: I work hard and smart. I have solved problems that have increased revenue and value to my company. I have documented all the value I've created for the company and will present it to my boss. At the end, I will ask for a raise. If I don't get it . . . I will start looking for a company that will reward me for problem solving and value creation.

Question #2: Is it really worth the effort to go after a monster client?

Blamer's answer: That customer is too big for us. We will just screw it up, so it's not going to be worth it.

Game Facer's answer: That customer would be a complete idiot to not want to do business with me and my company, and I'm going to find a way to prove it to them.

Question #3: Can I handle this timeline?

Blamer's answer: No way. I have too much on my plate that I already don't get paid for, so I can't add anything else to it.

Game Facer's answer: I trust myself and my team. We love a challenge. We will accomplish the task, because that's what Game Facers do.

Question #4: Should we really spend the money to expand?

Blamer's answer: We can't afford to expand. Let's not go for it now. We should wait and see if the economy turns upward in the future.

Game Facer's answer: Nothing will stand in the way of me and my success. Especially not money.

ACTION STEPS: GO FROM BLAMER TO GAME FACER

So I need to get you out of the blame game to get you to freedom. Where to start?

- **Face YOUR money situation.** Tell yourself and your loved ones the truth about your money situation. Yes, it's hard, and it might disappoint them. But they will get over it once you get back on track, and you won't get back on track until you get real.

- **Skill up about money.** Start slow or fast, it doesn't matter, but if you are going to stop complaining about money, you are going to have to understand it. Simply watch CNBC in the mornings. Or read the money section of *USA Today*. These two options are great for people looking to get their feet wet. Don't get overwhelmed—money is not complicated. At the end of the day, financial success equals assets over liabilities.

You want to own more than you owe. It's really that simple, and if you can learn what a basic balance sheet is, you will be ahead of most people you meet.

- **Let's talk about money.** Read about money. Talk about money. Ask questions about money. It's time for you to stop being afraid to learn about or talk about this stuff openly and honestly with your peers and those you admire.

- **Make a list of excuses.** That's right—you need a list of excuses. Every time you make an excuse for yourself ("It's fine that I lost that sale because I'm having a decent year anyway") or hear someone make an excuse ("The economy is in the toilet, so I can't expect to make more money this year"), write it down. And then *never* use that excuse again—not to yourself or anyone. You'll catch yourself making excuses and slowly but surely get yourself out of the Blamer mind-set.

- **Insure yourself.** If you don't have life insurance, today, at this very minute, *put this book down* and Google *term life insurance* in your local area. Set an appointment with an agent of a major insurance provider and buy a policy. If you have no life insurance, don't get caught up in term vs. universal vs. whole, just right now, *today*, buy a twenty-year term policy for a minimum of $500,000. If you already have insurance, it is time to give yourself a checkup. Make sure you have the maximum amount of coverage you can afford. I recommend twenty-year term life because if you really put part 2 of this book to work, life insurance will eventually not become part of your financial well-being. For now, if you don't have a multi-million-dollar net worth, buy as much twenty-year term life insurance as you can afford.

• **Change your friends.** Are your friends Blamers, Dreamers, or Game Facers? You need to start spending less time with the Blamers and start spending more time around the Game Facers. The Blamers are your *chronically* broke friends who are constantly complaining about how things never work out for them, and are full of excuses. It's fine to hang out with Dreamers, but don't spend too much time with them, or you'll get stuck dreaming and never executing on your dreams. It's harder to spend time with Game Facers if they're not already on your team because they're busy playing the game and have less time to spend with you, but if you can catch them when they have some free time, or offer to buy them lunch or just a coffee, you'll learn an incredible amount and get better at playing the game.

• **Get competitive.** Find the right people or companies to fuel your competitiveness and try to beat one of them every day. If you find yourself competing with a Blamer, you'll find yourself going nowhere. You need to compete with people who are far above your level, and beat them at their game. Never compete downward, always compete upward. Only then will you really start to move the needle of your net worth.

CHAPTER 3

Lifestyle by Design

YOU NEED MONEY FOR MORE THAN JUST EMERGENCIES AND RETIREMENT

You need more money for one simple reason: *freedom.* Financial freedom gives you the best outcomes and version of your life. It allows you to breathe, to sleep well at night, to stop fighting with your partner, to give you choice and flexibility. Freedom equals choices. The choice to do what *you* want to do. But as we all know, freedom comes at a cost. The cost is having the balls to *not* do what the Joneses are doing and, therefore, eventually being able to do what you *really* want to do. As my friend Grant Cardone (author of amazing books like *The 10X Rule*) says, "Pay the price today, so you can eventually pay whatever price you want in the future."

You'll understand how to shift your lifestyle to spend

more time working on the process I will teach you in this book. You'll be able to visualize the life you really want, and how to design your life to spend your time achieving that life with the most valuable resource on the planet: doing what you were meant to do. You'll stop doing what someone else has designed for you and start doing what you've designed for yourself.

Put simply, you cannot do cool things without money. You can't take your kids to Disneyland. You can't buy the diamonds for your twentieth anniversary. You can't buy any of the things or experiences you truly desire. Take, for example, giving your children the best they deserve. Think about it. What if your child has a talent for music or acting? She deserves to learn from the best and take a shot at making it big. You'd like to support your kid until she gets her break, but you and your spouse spent way too much time trying to impress your family and friends with fancy dinners, expensive gifts, and a mortgage payment that you really couldn't swing. Who really pays the price? Your brilliant kid does, because you frivolously spent your money and short-changed her dreams. So, your child ends up having to take a dead-end job instead of going to Juilliard.

Remember, money equals freedom. The freedom of choice, the freedom to give, and the freedom to help you and everyone around you reach their potential. Money is not emotion. It is not who you are, but simply a spoke in the wheel of your life. It helps you live the life you want or it keeps you from living the life you want. Your job is to design that life and then make sure to generate enough tokens to feed the machine. Some people have much smaller designs. Maybe they like to live in a tiny house on the outskirts of town. They don't eat out or take fancy vacations. It's all good, as long as that life is the life they designed and not the life they settled for because they chickened out and didn't go for their dreams. As long as they didn't let the failure of their first business keep them from ever starting another. As long as getting passed up for the promotion didn't stop them from trying for another.

IT'S NOT JUST AFFECTING YOUR WALLET

Not having enough money affects more than your wallet: it could affect your marriage, too.

Think about this: it's a beautiful Sunday morning.

Today is going to be a great day, you say to yourself as you wake up.

You want your wife to sleep in and you visualize yourself having a relaxing morning drinking coffee and reading the Sunday paper. After all, you are now an empty nester. Your children are grown and out of the house, and the financial burden of college is now behind you. Helping your children get through college with limited student loans was important to you and very costly, but you are confident that you have time to make more money and prepare for that comfortable retirement you've been dreaming of.

As you carefully put your robe on, taking caution to not

wake your wife, you leave the bedroom and quietly close the door behind you. You march to the front door to grab the Sunday paper that is always there, but that you rarely have time to enjoy. You open the front door, but the paper isn't there. *Very strange,* you think to yourself, considering that your paperboy never misses a delivery. As you enter the kitchen to fire up the Keurig, you notice it is already on. Someone has already made herself a cup of coffee. But who? The children are out of the house and your wife is still sleeping. Who could it be? And then you see her, sitting at your kitchen table, reading *YOUR* Sunday newspaper and drinking *YOUR* coffee . . . *your mother-in-law.* She is in her robe and hair curlers, and all your new reality comes flying back to you . . . *she lives with you now.*

Why? Because neither you nor she saved enough money to prevent this from happening.

Your wife brought the subject up so smoothly a few months ago:

"Honey . . . you know Mom is getting up there in age, and, well, she hasn't handled her money very well. I know we have helped her over the years, but . . . I think we should seriously consider letting her move in with us."

You reply with, "Honey, your mother should have thought of that when she was younger in life. Her financial problems are really not our problems."

Wrong answer.

"Well, what option does she have?" your wife continues.

"Mom didn't save her money. After she and Dad got divorced, they sold the house, and she has rented ever since. Now that she has gotten older, she just can't get around as easily anymore, and her cash is gone. She is living on Social Security of around $1,600 per month. She can't afford much of anything. I will not have Mom on the streets. She is going to move in with us."

You blurt out the first thing that comes to your mind, "We could pay for her rent at the garden apartments just a few miles from us. We could get her a first-floor one-bedroom with a patio. She would feel close to us but also have her independence. What do you think, honey?"

Your wife shakes her head. "Honey, we can't afford that . . . it's probably $1,000 to $1,500 per month and we don't have it."

She is right . . . you don't have it. You don't have the $1,500 per month to eliminate this situation from your life altogether. Had you done something different, like maybe not bought that Jacuzzi (which your mother-in-law will now take over completely), or maybe put away more cash over time, or maybe actually started that business on the side, or proved your worth to get a raise from your boss, you would have easily had this extra money. But you didn't, and time marched on and now you are stuck. And so, the inevitable happens: you give in to make your wife and your mother-in-law happy. Welcome to the next ten to twenty years of your life . . . with your mother-in-law in your face 24/7/365.

You could have stopped this and stopped the fight if you had just had more money. It's things like this that can rock marriages (and why so many couples fight about money). Emotions run deep and you might even get divorced over something like this. Wouldn't it be better to have another option? If you had more money, you'd be able to put her in that garden apartment down the street. Problem solved, without it ever having disrupted your household, your marriage, or your life.

Odds are that your parents and your in-laws don't have enough money either. In most cases, you will be called upon to fix not only *your* financial situation but that of your parents and in-laws. Think about this: Most of our parents didn't do a good job of saving because they thought Social Security would save them. The average retiree has a retirement nest egg of $10,000–$20,000. The average Social Security benefit for retirees is $16,100 per year. That's not much of a nest egg at all, and the burden of caring for these retirees will fall on your shoulders, just as it has fallen on mine. Both my mother and mother-in-law have virtually *zero* in savings and live almost exclusively on Social Security. My mother has monthly benefits of $1,300 per month and my mother-in-law has monthly benefits of $1,800. It's hardly the retirement either of them planned for (more like didn't plan for), and my wife and I are left holding the bag.

There's a very good chance that you will be called upon to help your aging parents in some way. Most people entering retirement have almost no savings. Wouldn't you like to be able to help out on your terms? If it's not in-laws or cancer, I promise you—it's going to be something. There will be lots of times when you wish you had more money. In the end, the result will always be the same: You either have the money to fix the problem or you don't. If you do have the money, the problem will usually go away or the severity of the problem will be minimized. Money does fix a lot of problems. If you don't, your life can change in an instant, forever. I challenge you to see your future before it happens. Plan a life that lives up to your potential, and for goodness' sake, stack and rack enough cash to keep you in the driver's seat of your life.

HOW TO BUILD A LIFESTYLE BY DESIGN

The goal of living a "Lifestyle by Design" is to *thrive,* not just *survive.* Sure, you could spend the rest of your life in a cramped rented studio apartment eating rice and beans and ramen, but that is not your story. You are better than that. You are a Game Facer. You picked up this book for a reason. You want more, and by reading this far, you have taken a tremendous step in the right direction. Let's keep going!

This Lifestyle by Design process helps to determine your path. It's the systematic process of understanding where you are, where you want to go, and writing it all down, so you'll want to take some paper and a pen in hand before we get into it. Visualizing what you want so you can get to work achieving it is the difference between those who get it and those who don't.

There are five steps to the Lifestyle by Design process: Core Values, Visualize, the Doorman Principle, Goal Setting, and Action. Really take your time on each step and don't rush it. It's important that you see every step of this process very clearly.

1. Core Values

Core Values are very personal to the individual, but they are critical. Whether you prioritize religious beliefs, commitment to charity, focus on family, the legacy you want to leave behind, or just your determination to hustle your ass off, you need to take the time to understand yourself and decide what matters most to you. I suggest you create no more than four to six Core Values. Here are my Core Values:

1. Practice daily rhythms to keep my family—both immediate and extended—together, strong, and thriving at all times.
2. Support my wife and my three boys in reaching their full God-given potential on a daily basis.
3. Force myself to reach my full God-given potential. Earn and keep an abundance of cash that provides my family with the freedom of stability and choice.
4. Work to improve my health on a daily basis.
5. Fight for the underdog and show people from all walks of life that they *can* have a lifestyle that they want and deserve if they are willing to visualize, set goals, and work hard to get it.

Now it's your turn. Write down what you stand for and what you're not willing to bend on. Core Values should be simple, shared with others, and unwavering. Here are some questions to help you create those four to six Core Values that the rest of your life will be lived by:

- What matters to you most in this life?
- What are you willing to do for your success?
- What are you *not* willing to do for your success?
- What other factors outside of making more money are important to you? (Family, health, travel, religion, etc.?)
- Who are the most important people in your life? What do you want to provide for them?
- What are your personal, nonnegotiable values?

By writing down the answers to these questions, you will start to see what is most important to you in this world and what will stand tall amid all the obstacles or little things that might get in the way. Take those answers and turn them into four to six statements—these are now your Core Values. Write them out clearly, and put them in a place of prominence in your home or work so you can remind yourself of them every day.

Your Core Values now become the foundation of your life. Once you have these in place, you have started the process of building your Lifestyle by Design—something to live by. Now you can start to get a strong grip on how much money you will need to pull this lifestyle off.

2. Visualize

Now that you've identified your Core Values, take time to think. Close your eyes and dream about what you really want. Don't worry about if it's realistic or how you're going to get there. Just see and feel it and take time to think about it. The important thing here is to *be as specific and detailed as possible*. Don't just say, "I want to travel." What are the places you want to visit? How often do you want to travel? Would you enjoy traveling for work, or do you only want to do it for pleasure?

I have specifically listed the following areas of life in the order that I believe are the most important for you to think about and visualize. But remember, this is *your* life. You are not designing my life, so make sure you use these as a guide and outline anything else that might be important to you. Think about what you want when it comes to:

- **Passion:** What makes you come alive? What do you need to have this/do this?
- **Family:** What do you value and what's important? What type of spouse do you want? Should they be a Type A personality or should they be more relaxed? Do you want children or not? Do you want to be the breadwinner or should that be your spouse? Don't go easy on yourself here . . . be specific.
- **Friends:** Who are the kinds of people you want to surround yourself with? Are they funny? Wealthy? Healthy? How do they make you feel? What's important to you in a friendship?
- **Health:** Do you want to lose weight? Put on muscle? Quit smoking?
- **Lifestyle:** Do you want to travel the world? Sit on the board of nonprofit foundations? Do you want to work for six months a year and surf in Costa Rica for the other six months?

- **Travel:** Is this important to you? Where do you want to visit? At what kind of level?
- **Education:** To what level do you want to provide and/or pay for education for yourself or your children or grandchildren?
- **Income:** The granddaddy of them all. What are your income goals? Run out the financial needs of your Lifestyle by Design. How much will your travel cost? Your living? Your spending? Go into tremendous detail in this exercise so that you have a very clear idea of what your desired life is going to cost.

3. The Doorman Principle

Once you have your Core Values and have visualized your ideal life, you need to prepare to make it a reality. But first, you'll need the Doorman Principle, as taught to me by my friend Rick Sapio. Some people can get carried away with their dreams, and in the pursuit of success abandon all the things that matter to them or make them happy. How can you ensure that you don't lose sight of your Core Values?

The Doorman is the protector of your Core Values. He lets in the people, activities, ideas, and relationships that meet your Core Values, and shuts them out if they don't. Everything that comes across your desk must be vetted by the Doorman against your Core Values before it even gets to "you." For example, in the early days of my business, I would take any opportunity to meet people and make new contacts. Now I'm more careful about how I spend my time: If I don't know someone or don't see a good reason to get to know them, I don't give them my time. And I no longer take lunch appointments. Ever. It's become a wasted activity for me based on my Core Value of work efficiency. If you want to see me, call my office. We will schedule a quick phone call to discuss opportunities. I don't need to waste two hours over lunch to find out that we are not a fit. I will gladly have a ten-minute phone call, but no more wasting time. Drop that Doorman in front of all activities and make sure he lets in only the ones aligned with your Core Values.

One of my Core Values is "Practice daily rhythms to keep my family together, strong, and thriving at all times." One of the ways I practice this is to have family dinners three times a week. The Doorman Principle makes sure nothing gets in the way of this. My Doorman won't allow phone calls, meetings, or visitors to get in the way of how I practice my Core Values. In my house, we all make it a priority to be at the table for our family dinners.

Much like a real doorman protects the residents of the luxury high-rise he guards, the Doorman Principle ensures that all your activities first pass the test of your Core Values.

4. Goal Setting

Once you've defined your Core Values, visualized your ideal life, and put your Doorman Principle into place, you'll use all three to set periodic goals. While your ultimate goal is to live the ideal life you've visualized, this is where you break down that grand vision into concrete yearly, monthly, weekly, and daily goals that will help you get there. Most people set goals way too small. They set goals that seem achievable and I set ones that seem unachievable. You need to push yourself to achieve more than you think you're capable of on a daily basis. **When you set big goals, it makes your small problems go away. You stop worrying about the little things that get in the way because your mission is so big.** We waste too much time doing low-value activities and worrying about insignificant problems when we should be focused on high-value activities, and conquering huge challenges.

I used to scoff at the idea of goal setting, until I realized its power and made it a daily habit. If you want big-time success in business, you must set big-time goals and revisit them every day. Your goals must be big and specific. Your goals must address things like how many employees you want, how many people you can help, and what your annual revenue is going to be. And yes, you need to have goals of greater profits and a larger net worth. The important thing is to write down your goals daily. Once again, as my friend Grant Cardone says: "If I set and review my goals twice a day for an entire year, that's 730 times per year. If you set your goals once a year on January 1, who do you think has a better chance at reaching them?"

Need I say more? Write your goals down daily, period, end of story.

5. Action

Once you have set your goals, you must take action to achieve them. Just do it, right? Action is the final step that will ensure you can have your Lifestyle by Design. **Push hard in the direction of your dreams. Push really hard, much harder than you** have been, and your Lifestyle by Design will happen much faster than you think.

Decide today what you want tomorrow, and take decisive and insane amounts of action to achieve it. Write your goals down every day as a reminder to you to not waste time on the small stuff. Go *bigger* from the beginning.

ACTION STEPS: CREATE YOUR LIFESTYLE BY DESIGN

1. Determine your Core Values.

- Write down your four to six Core Values. Remember, these are personal to you and your life, not what someone else has told you or expects of you.
- Set up daily or weekly routines to help you strengthen your Core Values.

2. Take time out of your day to visualize and set goals.

- Once you've identified your Core Values, you need to visualize your ideal life and set goals toward achieving it. This should be a daily practice, so you can keep your focus on attaining your dreams and make progress toward them on a daily basis. Spend ten minutes a day on this, either first thing in the morning or right before you go to bed.
- Get a goal-setting booklet. I love the "10X Calendar" by Grant Cardone. It costs around $20 and can be purchased at www.grantcardone.com. It has a place in it to write down

your goals in the morning and in the afternoon, which can help you to make your goal setting a daily practice.

3. Install your Doorman.

- Create your Doorman. The Doorman is the filter through which you will run all activities to make sure they connect with your Core Values. Develop the habit of stopping yourself before you say yes to anything and make sure that the proposed activity agrees with your Core Values.

4. Write out your Lifestyle by Design.

- What do the next one, three, five, and fifty years look like? Put the details down on paper.
- Set up time to dream about them every week.

PART II
THE ROAD MAP

CHAPTER 4

STEP #1: The Litmus Test

TO DRAW YOUR MAP TO SUCCESS, FIRST UNDERSTAND WHERE YOU ARE

Blamers don't care about their future. They have given up on the fact that they are in control and will use any excuse in the book to justify why they don't have the life they deserve.

Dreamers are still waiting for their perfect life to magically appear to them one day. They love to dream, but can't pull the trigger on any of it. They live a life of "someday" and that someday never comes.

But Game Facers build their lives. They take complete control of the process, build the road map based on their desires, and make it happen.

Now that you've figured out what you want for your Lifestyle by Design, you need to chart your course to achieve it—but in order to do that, you first have to answer a few questions to understand where you are right now. I call it the Litmus Test:

1. Are you living a life that is by your design and not someone else's?
2. What stage of wealth are you in? I refer to three stages: Broke, Accumulation, and Rich.
3. Are you in the right "platform" that connects to your goals, dreams, skills, and superpower?
4. What is your risk tolerance?
5. Do you need to take a step backward to take two steps forward?
6. Should you be an employee or an employer? (If you choose employer, I will offer you some words of warning.)

In this chapter, we'll address each of these questions one at a time.

The good news is that these questions are the key to figuring out your future and making more money. The bad news is, this exercise isn't easy and pain-free. It takes grit and guts. If I had had the guts to do the Litmus Test sooner, I wouldn't be in the business I've been in for over twenty years. For all these years, deep down, I knew I shouldn't be in the transportation equipment financing industry, but that I should be a coach, a teacher, and a speaker. Although I knew it, I didn't take the path out of fear. Don't get me wrong. Through grit, commitment to my success, the support of my coworkers, and massive action over a long time, my team and I have made a tremendous living and career for ourselves. I'm damn proud of it. But, deep down, if I had been honest with myself and done what I really wanted all those years ago, I would have gone to work for Tony Robbins. My first time speaking to an audience, I knew that was where I was meant to be and what I was meant to do. I'm a late bloomer. It's why I am *now* committed to writing this book and spreading the YOU NEED MORE MONEY message so you can learn from my mistakes (and so I get to do what I'm really meant to do—help you!).

The greatest gift the Litmus Test gives you is the permission to do what you are meant to do. That's not only great news for your happiness, but it's also how you make more money: when the work doesn't feel like work—when you are at true and total peace.

The other thing the Litmus Test does is help you to determine your risk tolerance. We'll talk about how risk is solved through research and analysis, but also how to use your risk tolerance to determine whether or not you should go into business for yourself. Don't worry—you can still make more money without becoming a full-fledged entrepreneur. Sounds like a plan (more like a road map), right? Good. Let's roll!

HOW BIG DO YOU NEED TO GO?

Now that you've have created your Core Values (the building blocks of your Lifestyle by Design), visualized what you want and how you want to live, we need to determine how much money it will take you to live this way. We'll need to calculate the difference between the life you want (and maybe you think you're living) and the wages you are bringing in.

It's time to get truthful about your monthly expenses and determine the cost of living your current lifestyle. Remember, Game Facers are not afraid of the truth. Use my categories as a guide. Break down what each of these expenses cost you each month. These are common categories that affect most of us. If you have more, add them in. If you don't have some of these expenses, just put $0 in that category. These are the categories I use for my actual budget.

Your monthly income is: $ _____
(this represents your take-home pay, after taxes)
Your monthly expenses are:
   Mortgage/rent (including property taxes): _____
   Home/renters insurance: _____
   Auto:
     • Car payment(s): _____
     • Car insurance: _____
     • Car fuel: _____
   Birthday gifts for others: _____
   Clothes: _____
   College savings: _____
   Dog grooming: _____
   Food:
     • Groceries at home: _____

STEP #1: THE LITMUS TEST

- Dining out: _____
Health insurance: _____
Housekeeper: _____
Life insurance: _____
Lawn care: _____
Music lessons: _____
Pool cleaner: _____
Retirement savings: _____
Schooling:
- Tuition: _____
- School tutor: _____
- School activities: _____
- School supplies: _____
Select sports:
- Registration fees: _____
- Travel for select sports: _____
Toy payments (boats, ATV, etc.):
- Payment for toys: _____
- Fuel for toys: _____
- Insurance for toys: _____
Utilities:
- Gas: _____
- Electric: _____
- Water: _____
Vacations: _____

MY TOTAL MONTHLY EXPENSES ARE: _____

You have now determined how much money you need to live your current lifestyle. Take this amount and multiply it by twelve. You now have the annual income you need to produce, after taxes, to live your current lifestyle. This simple exercise is so rarely done by most people. **We think we have an idea of what our lifestyle costs, but when we actually put it down on paper, we often realize we need more money . . . a lot more money.** I'm proud of you. You just did more to understand your financial needs than most people. You moved closer to Game Facer status.

ARE YOU IN THE RIGHT PLATFORM?

Now that we know your monthly expenses, we're going to need to evaluate if you're in the right industry, or what some call career path, but what I call your "platform." Your platform is the industry you have chosen or will choose. Are you in the right platform to achieve your Lifestyle by Design? Because if you are not, you might need to take a step back before you step forward. You might be in the right place with your skills, but working in the wrong place, in the wrong platform.

Your skills are only maximized to earn more money if you're using them in the right platform. It's important to figure out: *am I in the right platform?* You may be the world's greatest sandwich maker at Subway and dream of having a Lambo in the driveway, but unfortunately you're in the wrong platform. You may be in the car business and be the top salesperson at your dealership every month, and selling twenty cars a month can make you a nice living. But you know every month your compensation plan is subject to change, that the management is going to cut you back if you make too much. The platform you choose has to give you the ability to achieve your Lifestyle by Design.

The first thing you want to do is take a look around your industry and ask yourself:

Are there people in my platform who are currently achieving what I want, and making the kind of money I need to live my Lifestyle by Design?

In my personal example, I knew there was money in the equipment financing industry. I could see that people were making good money in the industry. Besides, anytime banks are heavily involved in a platform, you can rest assured there's money in it. I knew that the large publicly traded banks had the money but they didn't have the gritty hustle I did; therefore, I could out-hustle them and do well for myself—and I did. However, over twenty years later, the equipment financing industry has not changed at all, and many of the people who were starting to get lazy when I started are now on the door of retirement without a new infusion of young talent. The same is true in many industries. If you think the big money only lives in start-up social media platforms or in high tech, you are wrong. In fact, it might surprise you to learn that in the next decade, many of the old, once-boring industries will make a comeback and create tons of amazing wealth opportunities for Game Facers. These are industries such as:

- Banking
- Insurance
- Real estate
- Transportation/Logistics
- Manufacturing

These industries are filled with gray-haired management that are soon to be put out to pasture. They are working to retire, and many of them are simply trying to not get fired before they have barely enough to live on in retirement. This creates an amazing opportunity for Game Facers of any age to come in, take over their accounts, grow them, and make a lot of money. Add to this that many of these industries are behind the times in terms of marketing, storytelling, social media, advertising, and company culture, and you see that they are ripe for takeover by hustlers with skills—by the Game Facers.

Before choosing your platform, make sure someone inside it is achieving what you want to achieve. The masses inside the platform don't have to meet all your criteria, but someone on the inside should. Do you have the ability through your network or your pure gritty hustle to hook up with the people who are currently winning in the platform you want to go into? As we discussed, having successful people around you in your platform is *vital*. If you're not following a proven producer, you might be betting on a false promise. The reason that so many people are terrified of picking a platform is because they really haven't seen anyone win in it. If you can't see anyone winning in your current platform, it's time to get busy finding successful people and following them to their platform.

Only enter or stay in a platform if you can follow someone else's lead. Mark Zuckerberg, the founder of Facebook, might disagree with that idea, but he's 1 in 100 million. If you think you're that 1 in 100 million, go ahead, knock yourself out. Start something from scratch. Create something that has never existed before. But most of us have a better shot at success by following the odds. That's what I did. I went where the money was and carved out my own piece of the American pie. I suggest you do the same—follow the money and don't buy into a lie fed to you by some underachieving manager.

Another thing to consider when evaluating your platform: does the platform have longevity or is it a flash in the pan? If you don't believe in the importance of timing, just ask an Uber driver. The original Uber drivers who started with the company early made a lot of money. But within a very short period of time, competition and saturation flooded the space, and now most Uber drivers will make less money this year than they did last year. It started off as a great platform to make money, but no longer has that same advantage for the masses. It is a great fit for a side hustle, but it is no longer the road to riches that the original drivers thought it would be.

Meanwhile, here are just a few platforms that aren't going away anytime soon:

- Writing, storytelling, and video editing. These are only getting stronger in light of the impact of social media.
- Medicine/Health care
- Housing for all age groups
- Insurance
- Transportation
- Banking/Finance

And for the Game Facer who wants to be at the cutting edge:

- Cyber security
- Artificial intelligence
- Virtual reality
- Automation of any kind

These industries are going to change the way our world looks at everything. I suggest you look very carefully at them and see if your skill set and Lifestyle by Design might be suited for them.

Maybe your Lifestyle by Design matches with one of these industries and you are in the right place! Your current platform might not be on this list, and that's okay, too. Just do an honest evaluation of whether your platform's time is over or if it has a tremendous upside.

Ask yourself: "Am I in the correct platform to achieve my Lifestyle by Design?"

WHAT IS YOUR RISK/REWARD TOLERANCE?

Being afraid of risk will cost you money over time. But fear of making money is not real. It's just a trick that your brain plays on you. Your interpretation of risk is 100 percent connected to the amount of research and analysis you do.

Let me give you an example: When a friend of mine introduced me to a private equity investment opportunity, I was scared of the risk involved. I didn't know anything about private equity, and therefore it seemed very risky to me. The private equity company specialized in investing in early and small health care technology companies, but the idea of investing in these kinds of companies was just so foreign to me. I didn't understand the business and because of that I was nervous. My friend had already done a few investments with this group and all had paid him back handsomely. In order to evaluate the risk of this investment I had to do more research and analysis. I have trained myself to conduct massive research and analysis before I pull the trigger on any investment. This unyielding process forces my brain to look at risk and reward differently. After the research and analysis are complete, if the data and my gut feeling of the deal still produce tremendous risk, I pass.

So, I didn't just take my friend's word for the success in the private equity deal; I researched it. I called my family friend, another private equity guy, and ran it by him. I ran it by my CPA and my attorney. I Googled article after article about private equity. I researched and analyzed the heck out of it *before* I invested in it. I made sure to have a thorough understanding of the entire deal. The pros and the cons. The potential payout and the potential loss. All that research and analysis provided me with clarity. That knowledge removed my doubt and fear of the risk, and made the decision to pull the trigger and invest easy.

The reason risk makes you nervous is that you are unsure. The reason you are unsure is that you have not done enough research to determine what the correct decision is. The most financially secure people I know are willing to continue to make moves in what most other people would deem highly risky ventures. But for them, there is little or no uncertainty. Why? Because they are playing to their strengths. They have done extensive research, gathered the facts, factored the potential losses into their calculation, and maybe hedged their bets, and so the decision becomes crystal clear. Why do successful real estate developers continue to buy more property, and continue to build up their portfolio by purchasing more property? Because they have done their homework, tested the market, and come to a conclusion about how to manage the situation. The fear of risk lives with those people who have taken neither the time nor the effort to understand the data—every inch of it—and therefore are still uncertain.

We all perceive risk differently. If you were single and living in a studio apartment with total bills of $2,000 per month, your risk tolerance might be different than if you were married with a big mortgage and two kids in college. But in either case, doing research and analysis is the key to understanding risk and enabling yourself to make big moves with confidence.

I will never forget a meeting I had with a billionaire in Dallas last year. He wanted to explore the possibility of investing in my business. But after about an hour, it became clear that he was not interested in investing in CFF. He wanted to finance subprime credit, and my company only finances prime credit borrowers. Because we only finance business owners with good credit, our yields are smaller than subprime, but he was looking for bigger yields. After I explained that I didn't like subprime financing because of the increased risk attached to it, he said the magic words that I will never forget:

"Matt, you are a smart guy, with a good business, but never forget something . . . my definition of risk and your definition of risk are two very different things."

His statement stopped me in my tracks. He was right. His superior understanding of the industry actually made subprime financing *attractive* to him. He had run a publicly traded subprime auto finance company and retired at the age of forty-four when he cashed in his stock for just shy of $1 billion. His view of that type of business, through his experience and his research and analysis, allowed him to view the subprime financing business in some ways as *less* risky than the prime financing business. In short, his view of risk was so different from mine, he used it to become a billionaire—and I didn't.

That meeting opened my eyes. I took his advice and started deep research and analysis into the subprime equipment financing space. After a few months of reading, asking questions, and reviewing actual data, I formed a new company called Fresh

Start Equipment Financing, Inc. Fresh Start, owned 100 percent by me, now offers subprime financing for businesses wanting to buy transportation equipment. You didn't think I would just take a billionaire's suggestion and not do my research and analysis, did you? Of course not. His words forced me to work harder and to do more research and analysis into my business and into the subprime financing industry. So now I'm in both the prime financing and the subprime financing of the transportation equipment business and I think Fresh Start, my subprime business, alone will do $50 million in a few years.

Force yourself to do the research and analysis phase until you have so much data that your perception of risk is fully tested. After that phase is done, you might come up with the same conclusion regarding risk. But in some cases, you might change your understanding of the risk, and then pull the trigger on a new venture or investment or career.

You should ask yourself before pulling the trigger: If I am wrong about this, what's the worst that can happen? Am I financially in a position to handle that outcome? Understanding the consequences is part of your research and analysis and will help to determine your choice. But when assessing the risk, you have to factor in not just what you could stand to lose by taking a chance, but also what you might miss out on if you don't. We all have that uncle who wishes that he bought that corner lot twenty years ago. He says every time he drives by it, "If I had only bought that lot . . . think of what it would be worth today!" I have been that uncle way too many times and my financial wealth has suffered from it. I knew that all the kids were crazy about Under Armour clothes when the stock was $23 a share. It has since gone as high as $120. But I didn't act on it—I was uncertain. Would Nike come in and kill Under Armour? Would it be a fad? Did I ask anyone? Nope. Did I call anyone? Nope. Did I ask any of my friends in Baltimore if they had any opinions or information about the Baltimore-based company? Nope. I just watched the stock go to $120 and then I said, "Well, I missed that one . . . again."

How do you determine your own risk tolerance? Ask yourself: Are you willing or interested in doing the research? Once you've done that research and analysis, are you still feeling uncertain or concerned? Then you're probably not willing to tolerate the risk. Or are you feeling confident, because you know exactly what to do? Bingo. By continuing to do research, continuing to dig, you'll eventually determine whether or not you can tolerate the risk.

You must understand whether you are the captain or the passenger. Not everyone needs to be the lead developer on a new apartment complex. Sometimes, you can simply be a passive investor. Just put up your money and let it ride on the backs of others. Just make sure you do your research and analysis here, too. You'll want to be sure that you're working with credible experts who are trustworthy and have solid credentials and a winning track record. That's how I like to play the real estate game. I leave it to the experts to do their development thing, their zoning thing, their construction cycle thing, their marketing and rental thing, and I just put up my money and collect a check each month. It's good enough for me to be the passenger on that deal because I'm the captain in my business. I don't need to be the captain of all of my investments and neither do you. But in either case, you must do the research and analysis required to provide an answer that connects to your risk tolerance.

TAKE A STEP BACK TO TAKE TWO STEPS FORWARD

The legendary speaker Jim Rohn once said, "You can't see the picture when you're inside the frame."

Sometimes, you might be so wrapped up in your current money situation that you can't see the whole picture. You might need to take a step back to see all the possibilities for your life. Taking one step back in order to take two steps forward is something not many people would do in order to be able to lead the life they want to live. But as we've established, that is not you. You want to live your Lifestyle by Design and you are willing to do anything to get it, right? Well, you might need to make a move backward so you can leap into a bigger, more profitable future.

Take for example the bartender who makes $300 a night at a hot spot in New York City. That's good money to them, and could be hard to give up, and that is why you see so many people who start in the restaurant or strip club business and can't leave it. They get used to the short-term money and can't make the sacrifice of taking a step back to make giant leaps forward in their future. That bartender might really want to be a dentist or doctor or plastic surgeon, but because she's making such good money as a bartender, she's not willing to take a step back and take a pay cut to go back to school and pursue her dreams.

When you're sitting on a little money, you might be more willing to take that step back because you can supplement your lower income with your savings. Once again, it allows you the freedom to have a choice. It also raises your risk tolerance—it's a less risky move if you have more money to fall back on. In the next chapter, I'll tell you about setting up a "reserve account," which you'll find to be crucial in giving you the ability to take a step back to return to school, or to start a business, or to just explore your options and find a better path forward.

I've seen this firsthand at my own company. Three years ago, Sean interviewed with us for a sales position. He had been working as a finance manager at various car dealerships in the Dallas–Fort Worth area and his income was decent at $120,000 annually. Sean had earned this income for a number of years and was considered excellent in his field. Then Sean and his wife had a little girl. When you go from single to married, or from married to parents, it creates an overnight wake-up call. Sean knew that if he stayed in the car business, he would miss most Saturday soccer games, not to mention school plays and field trips. In the car business, you often work "bell to bell," as they say, and as anyone in that industry will tell you, your family life is for the birds. Sean couldn't do that anymore. His Core Values had changed and they now included being able to spend time with his family, not just support them financially. And to protect this Core Value, Sean applied the Doorman Principle to make sure nothing got in the way of that.

Sean found us online because of how much content we put out on social media outlets and proceeded to do a ton of research about us. He asked friends if they knew about us, and this led him to speak to both current and former employees. When he interviewed with me, his mind was made up that he was going to work at CFF and watch his baby girl grow up. His research and analysis removed any fear of risk and he knew CFF was the right platform. There was only one problem: At that time, our compensation plan for a new salesperson from outside our industry was $500 per week, plus commission. That was going to be a *major* short-term pay cut for Sean and his wife and his new baby. But he was willing to take a step backward to take two steps forward because it meant he could spend the time he wanted to with his family, as well as eventually make enough money to continue to live his Lifestyle by Design, the one that would lead him back to that $120K a year (and then some). He knew there would be long-term gains if he took a short-term loss. In Sean's case, it paid off handsomely for him. In fact, he didn't take two steps forward—he took more like three or four. In his first year, after bustin' his butt, working plenty of late nights and weekends to skill up, Sean made every milestone event planned for his little baby girl *and* had replaced his income from his previous career. In year two, Sean had doubled his income and never missed an event with his family. In year three, he tripled it, and in year four, he looks to hit a mid-six-figure annual income. The money part of this story is awesome, and if you are willing to step back to determine a better course for yourself and put in the same amount of work as Sean in the right platform, it can happen for you, too. But the greatest part of this story for me is not the money— it's that his daughter knows her daddy. Money can't buy that relationship.

You might be making very good money working for another company and are not willing to take a 50 percent pay cut to go into business for yourself or make a career change. You might have to move from the "cool" department in your company to take over the lead in the "train wreck" department. But that is how you get your chance, your break. Sometimes you have to eat a little crow, as they say, to be able to leap past everyone in the future.

FORK IN THE ROAD: EMPLOYEE OR EMPLOYER?

Once you've found a way to take a step back, you now have to make some decisions about how you plan to move forward. Everything we've talked about until now applies to you regardless of whether you're employed by a business or own (or are thinking about owning) your own business. We are now going to explore if you should work for someone else or if you should work for yourself. But how do you *know* if you should be an employee or an employer? Thank you for asking.

We've arrived at the "employee or employer" fork in the road to determine which path you're going to take to make more money—and it's time to pick one.

Your choices are simple:

A. Stay at your job and find a way to get paid more.
B. Stay at your job and make additional money on the side.
C. Become your own boss.

Whichever path you're meant to follow, I will show you how to make more money in the following chapters. But it's time to make a decision. Let's do some critical, essential research and analysis: Can you get the money you need through the job you currently have OR do you need some sort of side or extra income? Do you need to create what I call your own Personal ATM? You must do the research and analysis, and the path will become clear. Here's how you figure it out:

1. Does your current industry offer you opportunities to earn what you need?
2. Assess value points: what can you bring to the organization (based on your skill set)?
3. Is anyone within your industry currently earning what you need? You need real examples here . . . not promises.
4. Are you currently bringing exceptional—not middle-of-the-road—value to your organization?

5. Do you have the money to make a change if you can't get what you need?

6. If you don't have any money to leave and go into business for yourself, do you have a network of people with money to get an idea off the ground?

7. What options do you have? Money always follows the deal. If you have a good deal in business—an idea, investment, whatever—you will find the money for it.

8. Do you have the skills built up yet?

9. Have you done the research and analysis required to make a change? (A mechanic might want to become a pharma rep, but have they done the research, analysis, and skilling up to make the change?)

10. Are you really a business owner or should you just skill up, bring massive value to the organization, and rise up the ranks? Trust me—the number two through ten employees at Facebook are doing just fine. Sometimes it's better to be the vice president of a large organization instead of the CEO of a poor small business.

Once you have the answers to these questions, it should be clear which way you should go. But here are the questions you should be asking yourself:

- **Can you make the money you need in a regular job if you deliver more value?**

- If your regular job won't cut it, do you have a business idea, and have you done your research to get it off the ground?

Everyone is now in control of their destiny. The employee now has more power over the employer than ever before. It wasn't always like that. The employee is not beholden to the employer anymore. Employees these days have the ability to leave because there are a lot more choices, and one of those choices is to do your own gig. If you don't want to work for anyone but yourself, you can make it happen.

According to a December 2016 article in *Forbes*, the richest star on YouTube is Pewdiepie. He has more subscribers to his YouTube channel than anyone else. He is ranked number one with over 54 million subscribers as of this writing, and his subscriber count continues to grow at over 10,000 per day. He has over 15 billion views and consistently gets 5 million views per day. Pewdiepie is in charge of it all. He has power with YouTube. He has power with his audience. He has power with brands and therefore with clients who want access to him. He has power over his money (he earned well over $15 million in 2016), and most important, Felix Kjellberg, aka Pewdiepie, has power over his own life because he is leading it by his design.

You don't have to work for a manufacturing company until you die. You have a choice. Or if you like having the benefits, stability, and salary that come with being an employee, that's great, too. But you don't have to wait to be handed opportunities anymore—you can make them. And employees that don't understand that concept are the unhappy ones.

CAUTION: Being Your Own Boss Is Overrated

The trap that so many people fall into is the one where they believe that being in business for themselves is a greater opportunity than being an employee. I'm here to say that in the vast majority of the situations, that is simply not true. Fifty percent of all businesses fail in the first year. Ninety percent of all businesses fail in the first five years. That means that it's often a bad bet to go into business for yourself.

I know firsthand the difficulties of running a company. At my company in 2015 and 2016, we "torched" it. What do I mean by torching it? We decided to completely overhaul the business and reconnect to our company culture, our mission statement, and our Core Values, and we rebuilt our management team. During this torching process we said good-bye to a number of employees. They simply didn't like the new company culture that I was determined to implement. They didn't like that we hired a new vice president of sales and a new vice president of operations and a new vice president of finance and that they had to report directly to them. And they absolutely hated the fact that I put in place an employment agreement that made it very clear that although they could go into business for themselves and even compete against us in the marketplace, they could not take our clients, dealers, or vendors with them.

When I launched the employment contract to the group, I gave everyone plenty of time to review it with their family, friends, and attorneys. But one day before the signing deadline, an employee who had been with me for twelve years, earned $567,000 in personal annual income at the time, and had consistently been one of my top five salespeople came into my office and said, "You know that I'm not going to sign that employment agreement." I said, "That's going to be a problem."

He went on to tell me that he'd been with me for twelve years and that we could work out some sort of an arrangement in which he didn't have to sign it, but could still keep his job. I told him that there would be no side deals and he had until noon the following day to sign the agreement. The following morning, he came into my office and once again said that he wasn't going to sign the agreement, and this time also said that he was going to go out on his own and start his own equipment finance company. I wished him the best and handed him a box. He packed his desk, and just like that, after twelve years, he left his almost $570,000-a-year job to go into business for himself. By the end of our torch, three additional competing equipment finance companies were created by former employees of my company.

It was the worst decision he could have possibly made. The idea that he would replace the $567,000 personal income as a one-man band, without an IT department, a marketing department, a finance department, an operations department, or a meaningful brand in the marketplace, was ludicrous. He's now working out of his home office, scouring the marketplace for low-level leads with financing options that pale in comparison to the financing options and support that he had when he was employed with us.

I'm not angry or bitter about it. I didn't sue him, and I didn't go after him; in fact, if there's any way that I can actually help him be successful, I will. But best-case scenario? He'll probably make 50 percent of the income that he would have working for me, and he will have to do 100 percent of all the support necessary to be successful. He will have to be the marketing department, the IT department, the operations department, and the finance department. It's a perfect example of why most people will make more money being an exceptional employee rather than being a one-person employer.

So if you're leaving a steady job to go into business for yourself, your first question has to be: *how can I replace my income working for myself instead of working for someone else?*

You simply have to do the math and some research and analysis:

- How many deals will you have to do?
- How much revenue will you have to generate?
- What will be your cost of goods sold?
- What will be the cost of your payroll expenses?
- What about your marketing expenses?
- What will be the cost of the capital equipment? Debt service?
- Can you get the funding?

- Can you be competitive in the marketplace versus working for someone else?
- How long will it be before you can pay yourself a salary?

Once you do the math, your decision will become very clear to you. Does the bottom-line number of being in business for yourself match the number you would have made as an employee?

Notice that I haven't even talked about health benefits, or 401(k) programs, or employer-matching programs, or company cars, or travel to unique places, or any of those things that most employers cover that will now fall onto your shoulders. So, do yourself a favor before you walk out of your current job: Before you let yourself go down the rabbit hole of how much you hate working for someone else, or how much you hate your boss, or how much freedom you think you'll gain by working for yourself . . . do the math. Will going into business for yourself replace the personal income you make working for someone else?

Still don't believe me? Let me lay out a couple of examples for you . . .

In my twenty-two years of business, I have lost many salespeople who wanted to leave my company and start their own financing business. But none have duplicated the success they had while employed by my company. Why? Because they fell into the trap that so many others fall into: They thought their success was based on them. In reality, as an employee, you must base your success on a lot of factors. When your sole responsibility is to sell a product or provide a service, you can be hugely successful by focusing on that one thing. But when you go out on your own, you are now in charge of accounting, marketing, shipping, human resources, and contracting—you are no longer just selling. Therefore, your time is now pulled in many directions, you can't focus on just selling, and your sales drop. I have seen it so many times. The number one salesperson thinks he can do it better than the company he works for, so he leaves and starts his own business, only to fall flat on his face. In order to win at the game of business, you must be good—no, *great*—at all aspects of business.

Consider for example a barista at Starbucks who constantly dreams about what her own coffee shop would look like, and how different she would make it from Starbucks. How the organic coffee that she'd serve in French presses would be sourced only from nonprofit coffee bean growers in Costa Rica and how many customers she'd attract. She gets caught up in that dream, instead of the reality of the $10,000 monthly rent for the corner storefront, or simply the fact that people like the consistency and branding of Starbucks. That brand has been created through hundreds of millions of dollars' worth of marketing and advertising and thirty years of corporate growth. So, just because you're a great barista doesn't mean you can be a competitor to Starbucks.

Why is it so much harder to start a small business than to work for someone else? Most people think that clients choose to do business with the salesperson that they work with, and that's simply not true. You may convince some clients to leave with you because of that relationship, but at the end of the day clients want to do business with the best overall solution for *them*, not with *you*.

Think about it. When you purchase something on Amazon, you're not doing business with Jeff Bezos, Amazon's founder and CEO. You don't care that he's the richest man in the world, or the fact that he wears a blue shirt to work every day. You want to know when Amazon is going to get your purchase to you and if you got it at the best possible price. When you buy something at Walmart, you don't care about Sam Walton. You don't care that he drove a beat-up pickup truck forever or even care why he founded Walmart. You shop at Walmart because it's dirt cheap.

Now, maybe you don't have to get into a capital-intensive business. Maybe you're in a "solopreneur" field as a Web designer, a videographer, or some sort of consultant; but, again, can you play to your superpower and still deliver the same overall solution to your customer? If you can do that, and if the math checks out, you should go into business for yourself. I repeat: if you have done the research and analysis, and you like the risk and the results, you should go into business for yourself.

ACTION STEPS: TAKE THE LITMUS TEST

- **Calculate your expenses.** You need to get real about where you are and how far you need to go. Figure out exactly how much you need to live your Lifestyle by Design.

STEP #1: THE LITMUS TEST

- **Decide if you're in the right platform.** Who are the highest earners in the industry? Are there many high earners in the industry, or just a handful? Do you have the right skills to advance in the industry?

- **Find some rich friends.** You've got to make sure to surround yourself with people who have already gotten to where you want to go, so you can learn from them. Ask them about platforms that they think are good for you to consider.

- **Your mission is to research *everything* from now on.** If you're making a switch or a big investment, have you done all the research possible to ensure that your risk is as small as possible? What other questions can you ask that you haven't already asked? Do you have a buffer of money to protect you in a worst case outcome? By asking questions and doing research, you can always zero in on your risk tolerance in every situation.

- **Employee or employer?** There are pros and cons to both sides. Understand the risks involved in leaving a steady job to become a stable entrepreneur. You may be good at your current job, but that doesn't necessarily translate into being good at running a business.

CHAPTER 5

Step #2: Get out of Broke and into Accumulation Mode

WEALTH ACCUMULATION: WHICH PHASE ARE YOU IN?

In my view, there are only three zones of wealth that most people reach: Broke, Accumulation, or Rich. I will briefly discuss a fourth zone called Wealthy, but won't spend too much time on it—that's for a different book.

First, we have to define where you are. Which of these categories do you currently fall into?

Broke: You don't have enough money to pay the bills. You have to go to work whether you want to or not to cover your bills. In real-life terms, you probably couldn't go more than a few weeks without a paycheck before your world would shut down.

Accumulation: You have some money saved up. You can take the pressure of making ends meet each week out of the equation. You are not broke anymore, but you are far from rich. But you are working the program and if you stick with it, you are well on your way to Rich.

Rich: You no longer have to go to work to collect a check and live the life you want. Only when you get to Rich can you fully realize your vision of a Lifestyle by Design.

When my friend Grant Cardone recently interviewed me for his show *Power Players*, I laid out my framework for the three stages of wealth. When I'd explained the stages of Broke, Accumulation, and Rich, Grant said, "You missed one. You missed Wealthy."

Wealthy: Unshakeable generational wealth, like that of the Carnegies, Rockefellers, and Vanderbilts.

To Cardone, Wealthy is indestructible wealth. He wanted to skip over Rich altogether to go straight from Accumulation to Wealthy. Warren Buffett money, Bill Gates money, Rockefeller money. Wealthy is having the kind of money that even if Wall Street melted or we were hit by war or natural disaster, your legacy would never be destroyed.

I can't talk to you about Wealthy because I'm not there myself, and this book may not be for people looking to get there. I know only a few people who would meet the criteria of Wealthy, but to hear many of them talk about how they operate, it's as if they are still in Accumulation. They want more, and can never let go of their Game Facer mind-set. Warren Buffett, for example, still makes incredibly lucrative deals. Meanwhile, the people I know who think they have made it are the ones who have not made it, and maybe never will. The richest people I know want more. They want more money. Some want more money just for their scoreboard and others want it to help their charities. I believe it is because they aren't done building their Lifestyle by Design. They have the freedom to stop whenever they want, but choose not to.

It is insanely hard to get to Wealthy, and you and I might not ever get there, but nothing should stop you from getting to Rich. By my own definition, I'm Rich. I am able spend time with my children and travel with my wife whenever I want. I have enough monthly income to be able to decide how much I want to work, and what I want to work on. Despite that, I keep myself in "Accumulation Mode." It keeps me hungry for more. I'm not done. I still go to work every day. I still bust my ass. I work hard on growing my company, writing, speaking, coaching, and I enjoy all of it. Once you realize the power of Accumulation Mode, it makes you dream bigger and shoot for more ambitious goals.

That's why Rich is a tough step to get into, because you have to set the standards for yourself. Most people who read this book will be in either the Broke or the Accumulation category, and as I've said earlier, jumping from Broke to Accumulation is relatively simple. It's much harder to transition from Accumulation to Rich.

When you create the standards for yourself of what Rich is, you must stick to those standards. Don't let anyone else tell you to lower them. If the needle moves, it should only go higher. Your target net worth should never go down—only up. For Game Facers, this is the fuel that drives us. The competition of moving up the financial food chain is the game we play daily.

GET OUT OF BROKE

Yes, being busted broke happens far more than we think. Sixty-nine percent of Americans have less than $1,000 in their savings accounts and 35 percent have zero.

But don't take comfort if you're doing better than that, because the way I see it, you're still broke if you have very little freedom (if any), and you're enslaved to your job because you need it to pay the bills each week or month. I will go so far as to say that if you don't have a minimum of $50,000 liquid cash saved up that you, too, are busted broke. The average small business owner in America today makes less than a family of four. The average family of four makes $51,000 a year. Remember, this is a book about money. Most of us would consider that broke. It makes no difference if you are self-employed or work for someone else—either way, you could be in my Broke zone.

But don't fret, because getting out of Broke is truly the easiest transition between the three phases of wealth. It's literally the easiest financial situation to change because you don't have to go that far up the food chain to get out of it.

There is another important factor about understanding how to get out of Broke: Most people who are broke actually do survive. They actually have a roof over their heads, they have heat, and they have running water. They aren't in despair; therefore, if they can survive on Broke and if we can figure out how to get them 20–50 percent more income, they will quickly move out of Broke and into Accumulation.

Here are my six (quick!) steps to get you out of Broke and into Accumulation:

1. **Admit that you are broke.** If you don't have $50,000 saved in the bank (after subtracting any debt you owe), you have to admit that you are broke. You need to look in the mirror and admit that you really don't have any money, and because of this, you don't have any freedom. Maybe you lost your money, maybe you spent it, maybe your ex-whatever took it, or maybe you just haven't put yourself in a position to earn more. Whatever your reason, it's time to get past it because you bought this book and you want to change. Be honest with yourself—cut out the BS you have been telling yourself and others. Until you have the amount of money I suggest above as liquid cash in the bank, you are in Broke.

2. **Cut spending completely.** I'm not talking about your survival needs. Please continue to pay your rent/mortgage, utility bills, and household bills, such as transportation, clothes,

and basic groceries. But the gourmet cookies you think you deserve, or the new pair of shoes—bye-bye. Notice that I didn't say to cut your spending by a certain percentage. I said cut your spending *completely*. Anything over your bare living expenses of food, shelter, clothes, and transportation MUST be cut to zero. Don't go easy on yourself here. Just because you *can* doesn't mean you should. Cut it to zero and don't look back. It will be a short-term sacrifice that will provide you tremendous long-term gains.

3. **No credit card usage.** Cut them up. Credit cards are one of the biggest reasons why people can't get out of Broke. Why? Because credit cards are not tools to protect you against emergencies. They are tools to allow you to splurge. They burn a hole in your wallet and in your financial freedom. Cut the dirty little bastards up and do it now. Do not keep "just one." Put this book down now, pull them out of your wallet, and cut them up.

4. **Sell stuff.** Once again, anything over the basic necessities must go. I know this sounds extreme but that is because it IS! Get rid of it all. A garage sale, eBay, or Craigslist should be used to unload the purse, the bike (unless it is your transportation), the extra furniture, the extra computers, cameras, and the like—it all must go in order to generate some much-needed cash and momentum.

5. **Save $50,000.** Yes, $50,000. I know it might sound like a pipe dream. You might be thinking, *This Matt guy is nuts. I can't pay the bills and he thinks I'm going to save up $50,000.* I

understand why you would think that, but this book is the wake-up call you needed. I'm not going to give you the easy way out (but by the time you finish this book, it'll be a lot easier than you think). I'm going to tell you the truth—the actual steps that I took to go from zero to seven figures in my savings accounts. Until you have $50,000 of liquid cash sitting in your bank account, you aren't out of Broke. In fact, many of the richest people I have interviewed say my number is stupid. "Ridiculously low" and "not even close" were some of the comments I heard when I asked them if $50,000 was a fair number. But they have already made it to Rich and you haven't. Use my number of $50,000 as the goal to no longer considering yourself in Broke. But once again, don't get all proud of yourself once you hit this number. All you did was just get out of Broke. The goal of this journey you and I are taking is to get us to Rich. And I don't care how you slice it—while having $50,000 saved up after you started from zero might feel really good, in reality you are just not broke anymore. I get that you might be thinking that even $50,000 saved up in liquid cash may not be the ideal number for your situation. In fact, $50,000 might only be enough to cover your bills for a few months. I don't think that matters. What matters is that you have this amount in liquid cash. It's a new level of power for you and I promise you, it will give you the confidence that you can get to the next level.

6. **Start earning more.** Ultimately, you don't have an expenses problem—you have a revenue problem. While you do need to

cut your expenses right now to start getting out of Broke, earning more income should be your focus over the long term rather than lowering your expenses. Earning more is your ticket to getting out of Broke, into Accumulation, and eventually to Rich. As you start earning more, it is essential that you don't start ramping up your expenses as well. All your additional revenue should go into your reserve account—which I'll say more about in a moment. I will talk a lot more about how we are going to make earning more really happen for you later in this chapter, but if you want to get out of Broke, you will need more money now. Pick up extra hours at work, or get a second job waiting tables or tending bar. If you are already a solid earner, then become a top earner by bringing more value and more revenue. Do whatever you need to do, but start the process of earning more now so that when I show you how to earn tens of thousands more, it will make more sense to you. Remember, getting out of Broke is the easiest phase.

A BROKE MIND-SET IS THE PATH TO WEALTH

Even when you get out of Broke, you need to stay "broke" in your financial mind. Remember: YOU NEED MORE MONEY. This is your new mantra. As soon as you get out of Broke, you'll start to get comfortable, and getting comfortable is disastrous to getting Rich. Comfortable is when you start to find ways to spend your money instead of to save and invest it. Comfortable kills ambition, and ambition is one of my keys to making more money. Comfortable happens when your spouse tries to convince you that you can afford the nicer house, or the second car, or you stop producing more value that you can leverage for more money.

I'm all for celebrating, but most of us take it to extreme levels that often are not in line with our money situation. The little costs now cost us big over time. Game Facers understand this concept, and now so do you.

Complacency is the death of wealth accumulation. When you get out of Broke, you might start to believe that you are now in Rich. But you're not rich. You're just not broke anymore. Big difference! However, when the pressure of being broke is no longer staring us in the face every day, we back off the throttle and most of us will start to figure out ways to celebrate. What are you celebrating? That you can now answer your cell phone in public because you don't have collectors calling you anymore? Yeah, I said it. How would I know the feeling of not being able to answer my cell phone in public for fear that everyone around me would know it was a collector? Because I lived that life way in the past, too.

Very few people in this world are in Rich and can afford to be complacent. What you are in now is Accumulation Mode. Accumulation Mode starts when your bills no longer come on pink slips, and you have a minimum of $50,000 liquid cash saved up. But you still need to be stacking and racking cash to get you to your real financial goals.

But most of us at this stage slip into complacency. We simply stop staying laser-focused on making more money. People treat money and their effort to have it like a thermostat in their house. Picture the thermostat on your wall. When the temperature gets too cold (*Oh, shit . . . I'm broke and will get evicted*), you go to the thermostat and turn the heat up. That means you start getting up early, working out again, eating healthy, dressing for success, staying late, grabbing some overtime, following up with more customers, working every lead, and reducing spending. You start to make smarter choices, make more money, and pull yourself out of the hole you dug for yourself.

Then what happens? You go back to the thermostat and you turn the air-conditioning on to cool things down a bit. You have kept the creditors at bay for another few months because of your increased efforts, and reduction in spending, and then bask in the cool air. You stop pushing yourself, start spending time and money on things you used to say no to, and quickly watch your results fall again. Before you know it, you're back on the verge of Broke again, and the cycle repeats itself, over and over. Congratulations, you have reached complacency, and you have tricked your brain into thinking you are actually doing well.

For some of us, the people who develop a Game Facer mindset, we figure out the pace at which we are able to work to keep the range of the thermostat steady and at a higher temperature. We have actually created a financial existence in which we never let it get too cold. Game Facers can handle the heat. I challenge you to increase your heat tolerance, and increase your range.

When down the road you get closer to Rich, you will be operating at an even higher thermostat for a few years, and then you will be able to set your thermostat at whatever the hell you want.

The moment you get out of Broke, you've entered Accumulation—that means continuing to behave as if you are broke, while funneling every additional dollar toward your long-term goal of living your Lifestyle by Design.

ACCUMULATION MODE

Congratulations: You earned your ticket out of Broke and into the Accumulation phase of real wealth building. You are one step closer to becoming a full-fledged Game Facer. Now we can get started on stacking and racking real cash, accumulating money in accounts so that when the opportunity comes to make real investments, you can. Give yourself a pat on the back, celebrate with a long (but inexpensive) weekend with your significant other, then get back to work. You now need to build on that $50,000 and turn it into millions, because as I have said before and will say again, the money has moved and YOU NEED MORE MONEY.

Let me warn you now. Your grit, your ability to stay the course, will be tested. Accumulation is the most difficult phase to get out of. It is hard to leave Accumulation and move into Rich. Anyone can get out of Broke, but getting out of Accumulation is a whole other ball game. It's hard because you will face pressure from your family, friends, colleagues, enemies, neighbors, and your own desire to get comfortable and start spending more.

If your own grit to keep at it is eluding you, it could be because you spend too much time looking to reward yourself rather than spending that time developing a strong competitive drive. Let your unbridled ambition kick in here. Every time you feel the urge to celebrate, close your eyes and spend ten minutes visualizing your Lifestyle by Design and think about how far you are from achieving it. Think about how much progress you can make toward your Lifestyle by Design by postponing your celebration. Develop a gritty discipline within yourself to work and spend like you are still broke. Game Facers have the grit to postpone celebrations and rewards in their business and personal life. Until you reach the time when it's smart for you to indulge, do everything in your power to never be worthy of the ultimate insult said about Blamers and Dreamers in the great state of Texas: "He's all hat and no cattle."

In the town I live in, I saw house after house get built, completed, and sold. The people who bought them took on major mortgages to make it happen. I guarantee you, most of them made small down payments and took thirty-year mortgages. According to some of my Realtor friends, many of these homes have not and will not be furnished because the owners don't have the money to do so.

I wasn't going to let myself fall into a similar trap. "Let the Joneses keep up with the Joneses" has always been my philosophy. We Maneros were going to build when we were ready to build. Because I put off buying a house for years, I now have the nicest one in my neighborhood, with a fraction of the mortgage. Celebrating smart (and rarely) can and will save you a ton of cash in the long run.

Here are the most common habits and comments I hear from people in Accumulation that don't have the grit to stay on the path:

"I'm good." No, you are not good. What does that mean, anyway? You are good based on what? That you can afford to take a nice vacation? You can go to a nice restaurant? You have a 401(k) or a Roth IRA? You have a couple hundred thousand in the bank? None of these facts put you in the "I'm good" category. You are good when you reach Rich, and you are Rich when you are living exactly the life you have always dreamed of, without a care in the world. Until that time, you are either in Broke or in Accumulation, but you are not "good."

"I'm doing better than my parents." Your parents didn't do that well. In fact, they didn't do well—they did poorly. Unless your parents were Rich (by my definition) and they lived life on their terms, by their design with no financial worries, they don't deserve your comparison. You don't need to resent them, but let's not use their results as a barometer to compare your results to. If you are going to compare yourself to someone, find someone who has *actually* created the life you want to live and compare yourself to them.

"I still have time." Time is not a given. My brother-in-law, John, used to tell me this constantly. He would tell himself that he had time to make up the gap, but time caught up to him. The sooner you start, the more easily you'll get there. In our journey to get rich, we are racing against time. Time is a factor to Accumulation and getting to Rich, but it is not something to be toyed with. When you say that "you still have time," you are lying to yourself. Get after it now and stop believing that time doesn't eventually expire. It always does, and you have no control over when.

When you are in Accumulation, you need to stack and rack cash—lots and lots of it—so that you can eventually make financial moves that propel you closer to Rich.

Let me set the stage for how confusing the difference between Accumulation and Broke can be. It was years ago, but I remember it like it was yesterday.

I'm in my closet at my house getting dressed to go to dinner with my wife and another couple, friends of ours. Once again, they wanted to go to a fancy steak house in Dallas, Texas, Bob's Chop House. We've done this exercise multiple times. It really should be a nice double date between me and my wife and our friends. But for me, it's a nightmare. God forbid I tell my wife and friends that we don't have the money to go to Bob's. As I'm getting dressed in my closet, I pull out my credit card, and I literally call the number on the back of the card to check how much money I had available. Answer? Five hundred bucks.

I have virtually no cash in the bank and $500 available on my credit card and I'm going to an expensive restaurant. Absurd, right? And the thing is, you know that you've done the exact same thing—saying yes when you know you should have said no.

We get in the car, go to Bob's, and we see our friends in the lobby. We're hugging, everyone's in a good mood. The maître d' sits us down at our table of four and I cringe inside as I hear my friend say, "Let's order wine!"

In my head I'm thinking, *Please don't order an expensive bottle.*

Then the wives say, "Let's order appetizers all around and we'll split them!"

So, now we've got wine and appetizers. The waiter comes and announces specials for the evening. There's Chilean sea bass and twenty-eight-ounce T-bone steak, all priced $40 to $50 each. The fun of the evening for me has now completely evaporated.

I can't even enjoy myself because I'm pissed that I don't have a pot to piss in and I'm still acting like I do! I'm stuck and I'm lying to myself and everyone around me about it. I just can't bring myself to tell the truth and stop the madness. I'm terrified that my wife will look at me like I'm a loser and my friends will think I'm cheap. I'm viewed as a hotshot entrepreneur! I should have money to burn!

Before long, I'm looking at the table and there's shrimp and salmon, two T-bones, and a second bottle of wine.

Just as we're finishing up and I'm trying to signal to the waiter for the check, our wives announce, "Let's order a bunch of different desserts and split them!"

At this point, I excuse myself from the table. I go into the bathroom, go into a stall, and call the credit card company again, just to make sure I really did have that $500 in my account.

On my way back, I stop the waiter, give him my card, and $460 later, including tip, I paid for the entire dinner. Why did I do that? Remember, I didn't want to look like a loser. I was the fancy entrepreneur! I couldn't let my friends or wife know I was really broke. I was a schmuck.

I go back to the table to everyone full and happy. The waiter comes back and says, "Mr. Manero picked up the tab."

My wife gives me a kiss on the cheek. My buddy says, "I'll get you next time!"

Next time?! I gotta do this again?

Instead of $500 on a credit card, I leave with $40 left to my name, on credit. According to my definition, that is flat-ass broke. And we can all agree that it's stupid. That's when I woke up and decided something had to change.

Many people play the charade like I did. Some do it while they are young like I was, but some do it forever. It has happened for decades, especially before the recession of 2008. It was easy to mask what we didn't have and BS our way around. In 2008, we all had a wake-up call. Now it's the real deal. Whereas a nice car with a dumpy apartment or a fake Rolex used to fool some people, after the recession so many people were forced to live on the truth. The economic downturn negatively affected tens of millions of people, with real financial pain in most cases, but it came with a silver lining: It made people reconnect to what matters most—personal happiness, family, friends, loved ones, and the truth. It convinced people to give up on the fakeness and focus on the truth. (Although, in the past few years, history is starting to repeat itself. The good times are back and so are the phonies.)

A few weeks later, my wife said, "Hey, the Werners want to go out with us."

I said, "We're not going to Bob's Chop House, we're in Accumulation Mode."

She said, "What's that?"

I said, "We're in stack and rack mode, honey. I call it Accumulation Mode."

"What are we accumulating for?" she asked.

I said, "For our freedom."

Lucky for me, my wife liked the sound of it and got on board. She was in.

"What are we gonna tell the Werners?" she asked.

I told her I would take care of that.

I called up my buddy and said, "We're excited to go out to dinner with you, but I'm not dropping $400 on Bob's anymore. We're going to go for tacos. I'm no longer in spend mode, my friend. I'm in Accumulation Mode."

I began to feel powerful when I said, "I'm in Accumulation Mode." Accumulation means "I'm in stacking and racking cash mode," and that gave me confidence and power. I promise you, when you start to tell people, "I'm in Accumulation Mode," the same power and confidence will flow to you.

I'll never forget the night I said we were going for tacos. You don't have to spend a lot to have a great time, and we did both.

The best part was at the end of the night, when my buddy took me aside and said, "Thank you for saying we're not going to Bob's. You know why? I couldn't afford it either."

You don't need to drop $460 to have a good time with good friends, and if you do, those may not be the friends you want to be hanging with anyway.

For me, when I started saying, "I'm in Accumulation Mode," the slipping back into Broke, the dishonesty with my friends and everyone around me was over. It allowed me to kick that dark side once and for all. I was moving toward the light and that light was financial freedom.

But how?

By telling *everyone.*

Tell everyone, "I'm in Accumulation Mode!"

You'll instantly see the power that those words bring, just like I did with my friend. But you have to have the guts to put yourself in that position. This also goes back to not being afraid to talk about money. When you break down those barriers and start being honest, you'll see things start to change.

Start saying it to yourself. Next time you're wondering what to do for dinner, say, "I'm in Accumulation Mode," and have a simple meal at home.

Anytime you find yourself about to blow cash on something you don't absolutely need, stop yourself and say, "I'm in Accumulation Mode."

It'll start to flow right off your tongue. Some people are not going to continue to hang out with you. But the ones who care about you, your real friends, those are the ones that will come up to you and whisper in your ear, "Thanks. I need to be in Accumulation Mode, too."

Okay, I think you get it, so let's put it into action. Here are the four key steps to stacking and racking cash during Accumulation:

1. **You must focus on your money.** Once you're out of Broke, you can now stop having to cut spending completely. But be careful. You'll want to celebrate, to back off, to take your hand off the throttle; you must force yourself not to let this happen. What you focus on will get accomplished, and focusing on money when you are in Accumulation is vital. Think of it like this: Remember when you were in school and you procrastinated on your term paper? The teacher gave out the assignment with plenty of time to complete it, but you (and I) waited and waited until the last minute to buckle down, focus on it, and finish. The result was often less than our best effort, poorly thought through, and most often a less than stellar grade. Perhaps you were "that person" who could wait until the last minute, pull the all-nighter, and still get an A. Well, good for you, but last-minute efforts won't help you in the wealth accumulation game. If you don't take the time to focus, plan, stack and rack, prepare, research, analyze, and then execute on your plan, you will end up with an F in retirement. And in retirement is where the real grades count.

2. **You must create a second bank account.** Please listen carefully to me: You can't have just one bank account. You must

have a minimum of two. Your first account will be your "op-erating account." This is the account that will be used to pay your bills and nothing more. Your second account will be for *every single other dollar.* Stop mixing up your stack and rack cash with your operating account. Your money needs to be separated. Because when your money is all in one place, you will spend it. The single biggest choice I made when I got out of Broke and into Accumulation was to employ this strategy. Because I'm self-employed, I was able to set up two accounts with our payroll company. I determined how much money I needed to cover my bills each month (we did this exercise already; see page 70) and that became account one, called my operating account. Every other dollar above my bills went into my second account. I call it my reserve account. It be-came the account that held my money for future use. Your second account is *not* a secret stash or European vacation fund. It is isolated for a reason . . . it is not to be touched. You're in Accumulation to get to Rich.

3. **Make more money.** Here it is again. Saving can only get you so far. If you really want to accumulate your way into Rich, you need to start earning more. Don't worry, we'll get to how later.

4. **Upgrade your network.** When you are in Accumulation, you will need to move up the food chain with respect to the peo-ple you surround yourself with. The higher up the food chain you go, the more opportunities will come your way. The odds of getting rich by leaving your money in your bank account earning 0.05 percent interest are ZERO. It will not happen. If

you want to get rich, you are going to have to make bigger moves. You are going to have to find and connect with people who support you and provide you opportunities.

Now, you're probably asking, *When does Accumulation end?* This is perhaps the most controversial part of this book. **You can't even think about leaving Accumulation Mode until you have invested or have liquid assets of $5 million. That's right, $5 million.**

How did I come up with this amount? Easy. First, it is the result of the 1X, 3X, 5X, 10X formula. If you make $500,000 per year and you are in your fifties, you should have a $5 million net worth. I'm giving you the number of $5 million if you're looking for a hard one, but it might not necessarily be that for you; it's just a suggestion. What it does need to be is 10X your annual income as your net worth, so that 10X or $5 million can be placed into investment tools such as stocks, bonds, and treasuries, and you might be able to then achieve a 5 percent annual return. Now, I'm not saying you shouldn't start investing sooner (because you should), but once you get to the point of having invested $5 million with (let's just say) a 5 percent annual return, it will end up providing you with $250,000 per year before you touch your principal. I actually think you should start investing in mutual funds, stocks, and real estate when you have anywhere from $50,000 to $100,000 saved. That's because only then have you reached the right mind-set and momentum to get to the next phase of wealth.

But back to the $250,000—it's not a bad income for most people to live off of in retirement, but that is your choice. I'd say only then that someone is out of Accumulation because that is ten times the amount that most Americans live on during retirement. Most people can live a nice life on $250,000 a year. It's not enough for me to live *my* Lifestyle by Design, but if you can get to $250,000 per year in passive income, you will be able to retire without worrying that you'll run out of money. But when you do get to that point, you'll find that you have the capacity to go even bigger. I remind you again of the principle of this book: I NEED MORE MONEY, YOU NEED MORE MONEY, WE ALL NEED MORE MONEY! Don't go easy on yourself. Push yourself to dream bigger and therefore live better in retirement. Every single person I know who actually has $5 million wishes they had more. Because for Game Facers, they know that if they can reach a major milestone like that, they can also reach higher.

THE POWER OF "I'M IN ACCUMULATION MODE"

We've now established that most of us are in Accumulation Mode, especially if you're reading this book. The ability to start using the statement "I'm in Accumulation Mode" will change your entire financial life, just like it did mine. This simple statement has removed all of the stigma, the guilt I had connected to saying no. Saying no to splurging on the latest phones and gadgets that in reality wreaked havoc on my future retirement. Saying no to trips for select soccer or lacrosse tournaments. Saying no to vacations to exotic places that would push me back years from achieving my Lifestyle by Design.

Here is what I mean: The average cost for a family of four to go on an average trip to Disneyland is $5,000, including airfare, hotel, passes, and food. If that $5,000 is put away for twenty years, at a 6 percent annual return and you added only $100 per month to it, you would have $62,824 saved up. So, don't tell me, "The children need a trip!" Many families take their children to Disneyland when the kids are five and seven years old. Trust me, they would be just as happy taking a road trip to the beach or to a fishing cabin in the woods at that age. Put it off one year and you will have saved the $5,000 from that year in today's dollars and almost $63,000 in tomorrow's dollars. Now, let's get really serious . . . if you put off the Disney trip for two years (that means you saved the $5,000 from two years ago of not going to Disneyland in your retirement account wisely and instead spent a new $5,000 on your deprived children when they are seven and nine years old), you will end up saving $78,800 in your retirement account. That makes saying, "We can't go this year. We are in Accumulation Mode," far less painful, doesn't it? By putting off Disneyland for just two years, you will have an extra $78,800.

The beautiful part of being in Accumulation Mode is that your worst fears won't come true. Maybe you're afraid that your friends won't want to hang out with you or that your status in the community will be lowered. You're afraid of being knocked off your pedestal. You're afraid you'll disappoint your spouse if you don't plan an elaborate vacation for the two of you. Nothing could be further from the truth. When I made the decision to define the three stages of wealth as Broke, Accumulation, and Rich, I went into Accumulation Mode hook, line, and sinker. I started by telling my wife, "We are not broke, but we are not rich yet. We are in Accumulation Mode." This simple statement, along with the funding of my reserve account, have been the two most important decisions I have ever made in building wealth.

RESERVE ACCOUNT

Perhaps the most important strategy to achieve my financial success has been the creation and execution of a reserve account. I mentioned this a few times before, and now I'm going to tell you exactly how it works. Keeping my mind in a state of constant "broke-ness" while stacking and racking cash has made all the difference. I created two bank accounts in my life. The first account is what I call the household or operating account. You probably already have this account. It's your normal checking account at your bank. Your paycheck is deposited into it manually or via direct deposit each pay period.

The second account is called the reserve account. This account, as you will quickly see, will become one of the single best decisions you have ever made. I have used two bank accounts for more than fifteen years in both my personal and business life and it has saved my ass many, many times. Most people have this backward. They spend a ton of time working in and watching their operating account and very little time with their second account, their reserve account.

I'm going to now show you how to turn this thought process on its head. You will now learn how to spend very little time in your operating account and a lot more time in your reserve account. You might think it sounds so simple—"duh, that's called a savings account!"

Well, you're kind of right. First of all, it is so simple, but hardly ever done. But what really differentiates a reserve account from a savings account is how you think about and use it. I'm going to show you exactly how to use the reserve account in a way that makes it much more useful than a regular savings account.

The reality is that most of us don't want to bother with multiple bank accounts and don't have the backbone to say no to ourselves or others. Therefore, we use only one bank account and we fund it with all the income needed to pay our bills plus a little more—and we spend it all. Your operating account is the one in which the revenue (your paycheck) comes in and the expenses go out. This is the account that most people deposit all of their money into, and because of that, the money goes in and goes out within a very short period of time. This happens because we hate to say no to ourselves or others. We just have to have it and we have to have it now! We cook the cash each and every month and we never get ahead. But that is not you, not anymore at least. Together, you and I have made the choice to get more money, and we start right now.

The reserve account method does not require you to fight against this urge. In fact, this way you're free to spend every dollar in your operating account. Burn it up. With this method, I want you to cook the cash in it. Why? Because, eventually, your operating account will be on autopilot and your reserve will be in place. The reserve account is where you want your attention. It is your security blanket, your armor, your protection. Now, the big question: how much of your income should go into your reserve account? The answer is simple: every dollar *above* your monthly expenses should go into your reserve account. Figure out your monthly bills (you should have already done this). Make sure that amount of money goes into your operating account. Your monthly bills should include ALL of your monthly expenses. That means you should have a few bucks budgeted for your anniversary gift, the kids' birthday party, or even date night. I might also suggest that you have an emergency amount in place each month to help you be prepared for surprises, such as a broken stove or a flat tire. Next, set up all of your fixed bills, such as rent, mortgage, car payments, utilities, cell phone, etc., in your operating account on auto-withdrawal each month. You should no longer be in the check-writing business. Every bill should be automatically deducted from your account by ACH/auto-withdrawal. This allows you to stay 100 percent focused on the two key components of this book: *generating more revenue* and *funding your reserve account*. Call the company you owe, and have their monthly bill put on ACH. Some will set it up for you over the phone and some will require you to go online to set it up. In either case, *make it happen.* Just set it and forget it.

Your reserve account will quickly become your power account. I promise you with 100 percent certainty, if you get your operating account on autopilot and you get your reserve account set up and start funding it, everything in your financial world will change for the better. That sounds like something worth doing, doesn't it?

Once your operating account is set up at your bank, go to a second bank—*not* the same bank that holds your operating account—and set up another account called a reserve account. You will now have two separate accounts: your operating account at one bank, and your reserve account at another bank. Why two banks? Because I want it to be difficult to get to your reserve account. If you have both accounts at the same bank, you will be tempted to transfer your reserve to your operating account if you come up short. *This can't happen.* Your reserve account should *not* have checks or an ATM card connected to it. You must make it difficult to tap into it. **Your reserve account should only be tapped into for cash flow–*generating* opportunities. It should *never*—I repeat *never*—be used for *non*-cash flow–generating activities.** It is not an emergency fund. It is not a secret stash. It is not a "don't tell my spouse" account. It is to be used to build you a nest egg that *you* will use when you have done your research and analysis on a future investment and pull the trigger and invest. The only time you would dip into your reserve account is for a moneymaking opportunity you can't pass up. I'm talking about those opportunities that might only come along two or three times in a lifetime. Examples of this could be:

- A piece of property that you can get for $0.60 on the dollar
- Valuable stocks way down due to a recession
- Special inventory for your business
- The opportunity to buy a business on the cheap
- The opportunity to invest with someone much wealthier than you

It should go without saying that before taking money out of your reserve account to fund an investment opportunity, you need to do extensive research and analysis to ensure you understand exactly what you're putting your money into.

Now, how much should you have in your reserve account? The old adage was save 10 percent of your salary and you will retire poor, save 15 percent and you will retire middle class, and save 20 percent and you will retire rich. This is just not true. This may have worked for people at one time, but it won't help you now. None of these percentages matter. You are going to have enough money in your operating account to cover your monthly bills based on your budget, and 100 percent of the rest will go into your reserve account. *Period. End of story.* If you don't get this right, you will miss out. If you spend your life working off one bank account in which all of your deposits and withdrawals go into it, odds are you will spend it all and you will never build wealth. Beware of the power of our brains to tell us that we can afford it, or that we can spoil ourselves, or that it's okay to spend it now because we have a big commission check coming in next week. Giving in to these thoughts will kill your financial future. I want you to have the FREEDOM your Lifestyle by Design creates. And if you follow my lead here and set up two accounts and fund them in the manner I described, you will be well on your way to making your Lifestyle by Design a reality. It's that easy, I promise. You just gotta set it up and execute on it.

DON'T SPEND YOUR EXCESS

As you make progress along your path to Rich, you'll have a lot of opportunities to upgrade your lifestyle, but only some of them are really worth it. I'm a huge fan of flying myself around in first class. It is one of the few things that I think is a bargain. Why? Because it is a hedge against the cost of time. In other words, if I spend a few hundred bucks more to fly first class, I pick up time. Less time in lines at security, less time getting on and off the plane. In most cases, I'm off the plane and in an Uber on my way to a meeting before the last person in deep coach is even off the plane. This might save me forty-five minutes, and that time is extremely valuable to me when I fill my calendar to the levels that I do, with money-generating activities that more than make up for the cost of my flight. The additional room, comfort, and better service are just added bonuses. But few other upgrades pay for themselves the same way. I could have traded in my Chevy Suburban for a Range Rover years ago, but I have three boys who play sports and I have coached all of them and their friends for years now, and I don't want to worry about things like mud on the carpets of my Range Rover. I like things to be simple. I already have enough to worry about without having to worry about impressing people with showy upgrades.

Trust me: at the end of the day, countertops are just something you cut on, floors are just something you walk on, and cars just get you from point A to point B. Once you are fully on purpose with your Lifestyle by Design and because your money situation has improved, I challenge you to think less about the upgrades. They cost a ton, don't always bring back the value on resale that you paid for them, and often add aggravation to your life.

MILESTONES OF SAVINGS MATTER

Rokki and I married in October 1999. She loves to ask me, "What day did your life begin?" because I always answer it with, "October 22, 1999." It's true. The day I married Rokki, my life as an adult really did begin. Prior to that, I was basically busted broke, trying to get a business off the ground (without much luck for years), but I also was incredibly selfish and self-centered. I was out for me and me only. In reality, I needed a push further than keeping food on *my* table and a roof over *my* head. When I married Rokki, and when we had our first son, Johnny Boy, in 2001, you can be damn sure that motivation kicked in and kicked in big-time. Rokki showed me how to love unconditionally, and in return, I have wanted to provide her with financial security and a steady stream of a ton of income. My other half is my best half, and I was 1,000 percent committed to giving her a Lifestyle by Design—our design.

Unfortunately, for many years, I didn't. My business started from zero in a one-bedroom apartment with a phone and folding table and it just wasn't going anywhere. It was a constant struggle to find more clients, hire more people, and make more profits. However, through all of the struggle, the hirings and firings, the lean years, I remember like it was yesterday when I had $10,000 saved up. I called Rokki into the office and showed her the bank statement of our reserve account and it showed $10,000 in it. Free and clear, we had $10,000! We both looked at each other like it was all the money in the world. We just couldn't believe that we had saved *that much money*! We really had scrimped and saved, and look what we had to show for it! We were committed to that $10,000, so we worked hard *and* smart. See, that $10,000 was the by-product of having a reserve account. Without a separate reserve account in which we put 20 to 40 percent of our gross income, that first $10,000 would have never happened. We would have spent it all.

The 10K Day is a day that I will never forget, because that $10,000 meant more to Rokki and me than the day I had $1 million in that same reserve account. Why? Because when you come from broke, big numbers like $1 million seem like a pipe dream. Why else does the great financial guru Dave Ramsey say you need a starter fund of $1,000? Because it seems attainable to most people—and it is. And if you can reach small steps, maybe, just maybe, you can reach bigger steps as well. That was the same thing that happened to me when Rokki and I hit $10,000. It was the first time in my life that I actually thought I could accumulate some money. The problem was, as I have said and will continue to say throughout this book, it was *too small a number*. I was coming from broke, so $10,000 seemed like a lot. But I was wrong. As I said before, having $10,000 saved up was great, but in the big picture of earning and saving more, it was just a drop in the bucket.

Now, if you are starting like I was—from zero—then $10,000 is a big accomplishment, but let's not lose focus of the primary message of this book. You need more money, I need more money, we need more money, and, in order to get it, we are going to have to *radically* adjust the way we look at success. So, while Rokki and I now had $10,000 saved up, I only celebrated for about twenty seconds, after which I turned up the heat and got back on the earning horse to get the number higher. You will need to do the same mental celebration followed by "back to the grind" over and over and over in your pursuit of money.

I would love to say that you can take a small amount and turn it into a big amount, but the only way to do that is to crank up the heat and watch the milestones go by. You will need to hit the milestone of $10,000, followed by the milestone of $25,000, followed by the milestones of $50,000, $75,000, $100,000, and so on. The key is to crank up the heat and our revenue-generating machine to a level that allows us to cross these milestones quickly. I put enough focus on increasing my revenue fast enough to blow past each milestone, and although I eventually got over the $1 million mark, it simply took me too long. Remember, I want you to kick the shit out of my success. I want you to win at the game of money faster and at higher levels than I did. Learn from my honesty here. **Hit these milestones, celebrate for a just a few minutes, and then get back to the massive effort to generate more revenue and hit the next milestone.** Until you have more than $100,000 in your reserve account, don't even think about cooling off and celebrating for more than a few minutes. The goal must be to reach $100,000 as quickly as possible. What you will do with the $100,000 and the amounts above that is something that we'll tackle later, but for now, the minimum number that you must have in your reserve account before you celebrate is $100,000.

Money is a lot like reaching your potential or achieving your goals. The only thing that happens is you realize you have more potential or more goals. The more money I make, the more it makes me realize how much more money I really need. Remember, most of our money goals and expectations are set by other people. Your goals need to be your goals, not goals set for you by someone else.

HOW TO KNOW WHEN YOU'RE RICH— AND WHAT TO DO WHEN YOU ARE

How do you know when you're out of Accumulation and into Rich? When you no longer have to go to work to earn income to live the life that you have designed for yourself. This transition applies to the primary principle of YOU NEED MORE MONEY: you need more money to live your Lifestyle by Design.

Your Lifestyle by Design could be, "I want to drive a truck for six months out of the year and I want to hike the Appalachian Trail for the other six months." You're in Rich when you have enough money to do that. You have reached your Lifestyle by Design.

My version of Rich is that I now have enough money to live the lifestyle that I have designed and I don't have to go to work every day for a paycheck. That road to Rich is far more difficult than you think it is. The vision of surfing six months out of the year will 99 percent of the time be just that—a vision. Rich people get rich because they worked for it, or inherited it (good luck with that). They didn't limp into Rich. The primary reason why people never get to Rich is because they never carve out a path to get themselves there. They end up living a Lifestyle by Design created by someone else. But this will not be you, because you are becoming a Game Facer.

As I said before, living a lifestyle of your own design doesn't mean that you *have* to be the boss of your own company. I have multiple employees working for me who live incredibly rich, satisfied lifestyles. They have a clear vision of how they want to live. They generate plenty of income under the business plan that has been designed for them. They have absolutely none of the headaches that come with running a business—I take on those headaches for them. I'm the one that has to make sure that the IT guy doesn't quit in the middle of the night and that someone shows up for work tomorrow. I'm the guy that has to create the surplus account to handle litigation. I have to deal with it all.

You might ask, if I'm living a lifestyle by my design, why do I do all that, when I could easily hire someone to manage all of that for me? Because I enjoy being an entrepreneur, a problem solver, and part of my design includes being a leader to my team.

You do not have to be the boss to get rich. You just have to figure out a few simple things.

My friend Stanley is the perfect example of this. He's the guy who hosts the poker game I've been going to on the second Tuesday of every month for the past thirteen years. Stanley is one of the rich guys I play poker with. Stanley is a Game Facer.

Stanley grew up in the small town of Borger in west Texas. As he describes it, it's a horrible place. What made his adolescence in Borger even worse is that his was the only Jewish family. When asked, "What was it like growing up as the only Jewish kid in Borger, Texas?" he answers with, "It really wasn't a bad place if you don't mind your senior yearbook being signed, 'Die Kike.'"

I hope that puts an exclamation point on the fact that he really grew up in difficult circumstances compounded by daily anti-Semitism. West Texas in the 1940s and '50s filled with racial slurs every day was damaging. Stanley grew up with an effort to prove people wrong. He worked hard in high school, went to college, then continued to law school and became an attorney. He turned down large corporate offers by major oil and steel companies because he thought he had to do it on his own. He wanted to prove everyone wrong.

He made the choice for himself by going into business for himself. *Stanley Latman, Attorney at Law* was the sign that he installed on his office door, in gold-leaf lettering. Stanley slowly built a practice, but he hated it. I've never met a practicing lawyer who's actually happy about what they do, and Stanley was no exception. Practicing law became a fairly unsatisfying platform for him. But the machine of life needed tokens, so he did what most of us do. He packed up his dreams, his full potential, and his superpower, and he just did what he had to do to pay the bills and support his family.

Stanley built a law practice with over ten thousand divorces and hated all of them. Stanley tells this story of how his three children always knew they were expected to attend good colleges. But there was a catch. He told his children that he would pay for college *and* postgraduate studies, they would have no student debt at all—unless they went to law school. If they did, they'd have to pay their own way. He was that adamant about how much he despised practicing law.

Stanley saved what he earned because he was scared of not being able to pay it all off. Not just his kids' tuition, but the house, the bills, and the retirement. At one point, his family hadn't gone on vacation in eight years. He drove a Mazda. All his lawyer friends in their Jaguars would make fun of him because they were starting to earn and spend while he earned and saved. Stanley was in Accumulation Mode and he was stacking and racking cash. Then he finally decided he was going to build a new Lifestyle by Design. He knew that his law practice was going to earn him only so much money and he was never going to get rich from it. So he began to study, to conduct his research and analysis, and become very skilled at understanding the growth patterns of the city of Dallas. He leveraged his relationships and constantly asked people questions like, "Where is the population growth within the city of Dallas moving? Do you think that people will move north of the city or south of the city? Are there any plans to widen Interstate 75? What type of office space do you think business owners will want in the next ten years?"

After he spent a few years in this research and analysis, he had his game plan. Executive offices would be needed on the north side of downtown Dallas along the I-75 highway. He went on the hunt for a building that he could move his small law practice into, renovate, rent out executive offices, and eventually sell. And that is exactly how it happened. He found that ideal building, bought it, and rented it out to 100 percent occupancy with a waiting list of tenants because the expansion of I-75 had started. And when the real estate funds came calling, Stanley was able to name his price to sell the building. Everyone wanted a piece of commercial real estate on I-75 and he was happy to sell his building to the highest bidder. Stanley, after getting out of Broke, staying committed to Accumulation, leveraging up his relationships for information, and doing his research and analysis to reduce the risk in his decision, was able to execute on his plan and move himself closer to the finish line of being rich—and he was able to soon cross that finish line. Because he had a healthy reserve account, he was able to use it to buy the building. He was able to use this money to get closer to becoming rich because, if you remember, the reserve account is to be spent only on investments that can make you MORE money. Then the buyers came calling. Stanley sold his office building to a large investment company out of New York who made him an offer he couldn't refuse. It was a huge windfall for him. He played his hand perfectly.

One day, at fifty-five years old, he put on his suit, went downstairs, had a cup of coffee, kissed his wife, Lana, on the cheek, and went to his office. He said hello to his secretary and his clerk and sat down at his desk just as he'd done on thousands of other days. His phone rang, he looked at it, and then and there decided, *I'm not going to answer it.*

He said, "I'm done. I'm no longer going to practice law."

He called his small staff in and said, "It's over. The cases we have will all be worked to the conclusion, everyone will be paid until then, and as of today, we are no longer taking any new business."

He went home that afternoon, and his wife welcomed him, asking, "How was your day?"

He said, "It was incredible. I retired today. We no longer have to live a lifestyle that is not by our design."

Stanley went on to invest his money in the stock market. He became an extremely sophisticated stock trader, and in the past twenty years, his net income has quadrupled. Today, Stanley drives and buys whatever he wants. He and Lana vacation throughout the globe with an affinity for exotic cruises on the Seabourn Cruise Lines, the Ritz-Carlton of cruises. Stanley retired rich. He no longer has to go work to earn the income to live his Lifestyle by Design. He lives life on his own terms. Stanley's story isn't about investing money—it's about investing in himself, in his Lifestyle by Design. I want the same for you. To eventually not have to go to work to have the income to fuel your Lifestyle by Design—that is being in Rich. The reason we already figured out your Lifestyle by Design is so you can understand how you finish rich.

ACTION STEPS: GET INTO ACCUMULATION MODE

- **Cut it out** You're done spending on anything else but your expenses. Once you're out of Broke, feel free to burn up the money in your operating account, but only because you put the exact amount you need every month in there.

- **Two bank accounts, two banks.** This will help you to not be tempted to move the money from your reserve account into your operating account. Do not touch your reserve under any circumstance until you're ready to use it for investing to make more money.

- **Get to $100K.** It's going to take a while, and you should definitely feel proud when you have saved the milestones along the way, but life and Accumulation really start at $100,000— and it's only the beginning. You're only in Rich when you have enough money to live your Lifestyle by Design without having to go to work every day for a paycheck.

- **Keep your broke mind-set.** This will prevent you from getting too comfortable. Keep the heat on. You are not "good."

- **"I'm in Accumulation Mode."** This is your new mantra and will explain to your family and friends why you're changing your spending habits.

CHAPTER 6

Step #3: Surround Yourself with Game Facers

DON'T GO IT ALONE

Most successful people work better on a team than alone. This is because the most successful people tend to do only one or two things at a superpower level (we'll figure out what your superpower is in the next chapter). Look at the yin and yang of some of the most successful names in recent decades: Steve Jobs and Steve Wozniak—Apple. Bill Gates and Paul Allen—Microsoft. Larry Page and Sergey Brin—Google. These are just a few of the tag teams of incredibly successful people whose talents complement each other. You want to find the yang to your yin. Find a partner you can trust, or a guru or mentor. The problem is, you may not always have that option. I didn't. I once heard Warren Buffett say, "Show me your hero and I will show you how successful you will be in life."

When you're figuring out whom to connect with or ask for guidance, ask yourself:

- Whom do I admire?
- Can I do what they do?
- Do I trust them? Are they the right person to give me insight on who I am or who I could be?

You wouldn't go to a marriage counselor who has been divorced three times, and yet we take money advice from people who have no money. You must find a money mentor—someone who has already reached the financial level that you want and then *follow their lead.* You need to find someone you can emulate. If you can't find them in person, find them in tapes, books, and videos. Since I never found a steady mentor or business partner, I turned to books, tapes, CDs, and videos—I have read, watched, and listened to thousands and thousands of them. That translates to thousands and thousands of hours searching and clawing to find assistance. Some of my favorite "virtual" mentors have become Tom Hopkins (sales), Tom Peters (management), and most recently Grant Cardone (sales training) and Gary Vaynerchuk (social marketing).

Here is a good checklist to make sure you're talking to the right people:

1. They must have something you want.

2. They must be more successful than you (i.e., if you want marriage advice, ask someone who has been married for fifty years).

3. They must be trustworthy.

4. They can't have chemical addictions of any kind—including alcohol.

5. They must be willing to help you with little in return for them.

Simple, right? It may be harder than you think. It will take you a while to find a few such people and even longer to find one who can be a mentor. That's okay, be patient. Ask around. Keep looking. You'll find them.

ASPIRE TO YOUR OWN SUCCESS, DON'T WORRY ABOUT OTHERS'

Here's a question I'm guessing you've asked yourself several times: "How on earth does THAT guy afford that?"

I've certainly asked myself this question in hundreds of situations. In my younger days, I asked the question with curiosity. There's a scene in the movie *The Pursuit of Happyness* when Will Smith's character walks up to a guy pulling up in a Ferrari and he asks, "What do you do for a living?" That was me, all the time, from the ages of twelve to twenty-four, always searching for guidance on what career path I should take to earn money.

I knew I wanted money, so I chose the hotel business to find my riches. It seemed exciting to me—the ability to run a hotel and be the big cheese. People would travel from all over the world to the hotel that I was in charge of. They would ask for the general manager and I would drop in to greet them and answer any questions they had. I would be the big boss who could make their dream trip come true. I pursued this passion first by going to culinary school and then adjusting my degree to hotel restaurant management at Johnson and Wales University in Providence, Rhode Island. It was considered then and still today one of the best schools in the industry. I heard some people say it was right up there with Cornell. Imagine that: me, a C and D student going to a college that was right up there with an Ivy League school.

Once I got there, I quickly learned that Johnson and Wales was where the poor kids went and Cornell was where the rich kids went. This turned out to be a good fit for me because I always looked at myself as the poor kid fighting against the rich kids. This mind-set has been a double-edged sword, and if I am 100 percent honest with myself, it hurt me financially. The chip I had on my shoulder against the rich kept me from asking for help, networking up, and in my deepest thoughts made me feel inadequate. Not up to par. Less than them. I felt like the underdog, the outsider. It *has* fueled me to be better and push myself my entire life, and is perhaps the reason that I have achieved a level of financial success that puts me in the top 1 percent of the 1 percent, but still—I really should have a *lot* more money. It's this self-defeating mind-set that made me believe I had to do it on my own, my way. This kind of thinking, if used properly, can create success, but it will also hold you back. You want to maximize your success, and in order to do that, you need the help of others. And in order to ask for help, you first have to believe that you are worthy. You may not have the money of more successful people, but everyone starts from somewhere. One truth I've discovered is that most rich people want to help other people get rich. You just have to believe enough in yourself to have the guts to ask for the help. Don't wait as long as I did. **Believe in yourself in all aspects of your life and ask for advice from people who have achieved more than you. You will be surprised how many of them will give you the answers you are looking for.**

While you should be on the lookout for successful people who can mentor and advise you, don't fall into the trap of comparing yourself to others and wondering what they think of you. Here's a more useful way to think about other people and their success:

1. **It's your life, not theirs.** Stop keeping up with the Joneses and start keeping up with the (Insert Your Family Name). Your opinion of others is a waste of your time because they couldn't care less. The wealthiest people I know don't care what you think of them. The least wealthy people I know care a lot about what others think. Remove your judgment of others and increase your judgment of yourself.

2. **Be happy for the success of others.** When others succeed, you can learn. Spend time actually supporting the success of others by asking them how they did it.

3. **Follow the money.** Connect with people who have what you want. Ask your successful friends out to lunch. Tell them that you are in Accumulation Mode and that you want more money.

4. **Attend conferences and workshops.** You can connect with and learn of new developments, and hear exciting ideas from the leading thinkers and practitioners in your industry by attending relevant conferences, workshops, and conventions. Better yet, if you've built some expertise, see if you can get invited to be a speaker yourself.

FOLLOW OTHER PEOPLE'S MONEY

I remember when I started to move up the food chain and follow the money. I started by asking the limited number of people I knew with money if they would help me. At first, I was bad at this because I was so hung up on my own insecurities and my low self-esteem. I believed that these more successful people would see that I wasn't as successful as they thought, and this mind-set held me back. Remember our commitment to each other in this book: We are moving past fake and embracing reality. We are now awake and alive and in control of our money situation and no longer held back by our past.

I started to have lunch with people—on my dime—and I would literally say, "I'm looking to network with highly successful individuals who can help me make more money." People were happy to take me up on the offer! The lunch appointments and opportunities opened me up to an entirely new world. One of the most valuable mentors I connected with was Norm Brodsky, a wealthy serial entrepreneur whom I met at an *Inc.* magazine program called Birthing of Giants. BOG is an entrepreneurial incubator of sorts that accepts only sixty applicants. I applied in 1999 and was accepted. The program lasted three years, and for one week each year, I would fly to MIT (yes, *that* MIT) and learn from the best minds anywhere. I felt out of place and I was afraid and confused when I got there. The other fifty-nine students were way above me at that time. They'd accomplished incredible things, and it showed in their confidence and swagger. Meanwhile, it was 1999, and my business was only four years old. I was newly married to my sweetie, Rokki, and I didn't have a pot to piss in. I remember putting the $2,000 fee and flight on my credit card because I didn't have the cash in my personal or company bank account. I don't regret spending the money, but I regret not making the best use of my time there. If I could do it all again, the first thing I would have said when we went around the room doing introductions would have been, "I don't have a clue why I'm here. I have no idea who read or didn't read my admission application, but you screwed up and gave my seat to the wrong person . . . *me!* I'm totally outclassed and in over my head. But I'm hungry and gritty and honored to be here and learning from everyone." Instead, I stood up and made up some BS about how well my business was doing and that we were going to take over the equipment financing industry. I spent most of my time there trying to impress others instead of just learning. I could have learned so much at BOG, but wasted the opportunity, and put very little of what I did learn into place when I got back, which must have cost me a decade of my success.

But back to Norm. Norm was one of the speakers at BOG when I attended. He was raw and street-smart (he even later wrote a book called *Street Smarts*) and I loved him and his message. He was all about common sense and was blue collar, which resonated with me. His message was a mixture of grit and hard work, but also of intelligence. He had a good commonsense approach to his decision making, but because he was a CPA by trade, he combined this with a hard analytical look at the numbers. He made an incredible impact on me, but after the program ended in 2001, we lost touch.

Fast-forward thirteen years to 2014, when my company made the *Inc.* magazine Top 500/5000 Fastest-Growing Companies in America, and whom did I see on the speaker list at the awards banquet in Phoenix? You guessed it—Norm. I may have missed the opportunity to connect with him at BOG, when I was young and foolish, but I wasn't going to miss another chance. I knew Norm was a cigar lover, so before I left Dallas, I bought him a $300 box of six very fancy cigars as a gift. I left the box at the front desk for him and they delivered it to his room. I knew he would love it and maybe he would remember me from BOG all those years before.

When I saw Norm and his lovely wife, Elaine, at the banquet, I went up to them and reintroduced myself. It was clear he didn't remember me, but he did get the cigars. It got me Norm's attention and some of his time.

"Norm, I need your help," I told him. "I've had success since we last saw each other, but I know I'm capable of more. I'm trying to move up the food chain and make more money. I want to improve my network. Do you have any suggestions for me?"

He said, "Of course. Once a year I have a cigar and bourbon night at my home in New York City for twenty-five people. I want you to come to the next one."

Boom. Connection made.

He sent me the invite a few months later and off to NYC I went. At that party, I once again showed my honesty and humility and asked people, "Who do you know in Dallas that I should meet?" One of the other guests said, "You have to meet my friend Rick Sapio. He is a Dallas guy and I will connect you."

Boom. Another connection.

An e-mail introduction was made, followed up by lunch and subsequent personal visits, and Rick and I have since become great friends. He has helped me tremendously. He has also introduced me to a few select people, and as a result I'm now an investor in a private equity fund that invests in high-tech health care companies. This fund might turn out to be the best investment I have ever made and has helped me make more money *and* more connections. Why? Because I dropped the BS, stopped lying to myself and to others, and started to get honest and ask for help. I'm begging you: follow my lead and do the same in your life.

Talk to people with proven and verifiable success. Ask for

advice. **Follow their lead. Model what they do and learn from them.** Don't just let the answers to your questions pass you by and certainly don't be phony about any of your experiences. Just keep asking questions and take action on the answers.

LEARN FROM EXPERTS

QUESTION: Why is it that every top athlete has a coach, but most businesspeople don't?

> **ANSWER:** While athletes are focused on developing their skills, most businesspeople don't think they need to, and so they never make it out of mediocrity. Whatever your line of work, you can only reach the pinnacle of your career if you focus on mastering your craft. You are still, sorry to say, an amateur. Today, experts get paid, while amateurs get crushed. Developing more skills in business is *not* something you can do without if you want to reach your maximum level of success. When the chips are down, it's your skills, your mastery, and the confidence that comes from that mastery that give you the grit to fight another day. It's also how you make the most money.

You need to put in the time and effort to understand every aspect of how business works, or you risk getting burned. Understanding business in today's world means more than just owning a business—it means you need some sort of expertise in everything from sales, legal, insurance, licensing, and accounting, to marketing, social media, human resources, information technology, and more. Even if you are not going to be an expert in everything, you can borrow knowledge from the experts who are, and therefore deliver more value to your company and your clients.

Whether you're an employee or an employer, you need to learn everything you can about everything that impacts your industry and how to make the industry work for you. And while you need to rely on stellar employees or coworkers so you don't have to do every job on your own, that does not mean you have the luxury of not knowing how every job works.

You increase your value when you acquire more knowledge (and we'll talk more about how your value earns you more money in chapter 8). So, for example, while you may not be interested in what the IT department does or you don't think it impacts your career because you work in marketing, if you know more about how IT works and how it affects your marketing efforts, you become exponentially more valuable. Ask to sit in on the IT meeting, take the IT manager to lunch, start Googling *How does IT affect marketing?* I promise you, one of the easiest ways to increase your value within your company is to spend just ten minutes a day talking to people and researching the areas that you don't directly control.

An important factor here is not to become bothersome. Just open your eyes and ears, and file the knowledge away for a later date. You don't need to start interfering in other people's jobs or announcing your half-baked ideas on how they could do it differently. You want to learn how it all works, not how to do it all, and you want to be humble when asking for information.

When I started at Hilton Hotels in 1991, I learned this the hard way. I was the rookie in the sales department trying to make a name for himself. I was a hotshot who, at twenty-two years old, wanted to learn it all and would come in earlier than everyone and stay later. I would come in on Sundays and watch how the restaurant worked. I would stay late and talk to the bellman and see how he would greet guests by name by looking at their luggage tags. I would work out in the hotel gym to talk to the health club manager and I would lean on the front desk and listen to how the conversation went when a guest was checking in. This all was cool to me and I quickly got noticed as a good guy, as a hustler.

But then I started to open my mouth. I would say to the bellman, "Hey, here is a list of the companies I work with. If you see one of their reps check in, let me know." I would do the same for the gym manager and the front desk clerk. Then one day, one of the bellmen said, "Screw you, Manero. You are not my boss. Get the hell out of my way." Shortly after that, the front desk manager asked to see me and she said, "I liked you at first, but now I see that you really don't know your place. You don't tell my staff anything. Nothing. *Zero*. And a word of advice: When you want to say something? You should go back to your little cube and start making more cold calls." She was 100 percent right and I never forgot it. Even now, when I feel myself opening my mouth and speaking when it doesn't belong, I get my ass back to my desk and play to my strengths: *get on the phone and start making money.*

CREATE A GRITTY TEAM OF ADVISORS

You're starting to recognize the kind of people you want to surround yourself with and take advice from. Good, because you're going to need them.

When I started my business in 1995, I was told not to trust anyone. I was told things like, "Only one hand works the register," and "Only you handle the books." It was due to this poor advice and thinking that I didn't trust anyone. I never hired a great accountant, lawyer, insurance agent, or business advisor. I thought I could, and should, do it all on my own.

WRONG. Sure, it was good that I developed my skills in those areas, like we discussed above, but it wasn't good that I was missing out on having strong advisors, and my business was suffering for it. I needed a strong team of advisors to support me and my business, and so do you. These people are on your team to make you better. *They work for you* and they must have your best interests in mind. Even if you aren't in business for yourself, it's still a good idea to get a team of advisors together. You never know when or why you might need them.

Here are the players to select for your team: an accountant, a lawyer, an insurance agent, a finance partner, and a mentor.

1. **Accountant.** Everyone needs this person. It is your duty to pay your taxes, but not a penny more than you should. You need a good accountant, either on staff or at an outside company, to help manage your income, expenses, profits, and

taxes. Find a good accountant, update them every month, and keep accurate books. Equally important is that your accountant makes recommendations for you. He or she must be a gritty, out-of-the-box thinker if they are going to help you maximize your profits. I want everything you do to be 100 percent aboveboard, but a gritty accountant knows how to deploy strategies that can help you drive your financial success into the proper lower-tax and higher-profit zone.

2. **Insurance agent.** Your insurance agent must be an expert in your industry because they should be making recommendations to protect you. Ask about types of general liability, product liability, life insurance, health insurance, downtime coverage, breakdown coverage, gap insurance, and even disability insurance. Make sure you have enough coverage so that your assets are protected in case of disaster. This is still important if you're an employee to make sure you're fully covered outside of what your company might offer.

3. **Lawyer.** You don't need a nice lawyer—you need a tough, nasty, gritty lawyer. Your lawyer is going to do the dirty work for you when called upon, and you don't want a wimp. You need someone willing to be tough and demanding. Be proactive in finding the right lawyer. Have a good lawyer lined up, and build a relationship with them, so that if and when an issue arises, you can call them and they will already know you and your situation.

4. **Finance partner.** Build a relationship with your banker or finance partner before you need them. You want your finance

partner, if needed, to issue credit and/or advice quickly. You need to prepare for this in advance. A finance partner can be your banker or an independent finance company. Either way, you need them to understand your situation and offer quality recommendations and be able to pull the *approved* trigger when you need it most. This is still a good idea if you're an employee in case a side opportunity arises that you need to act fast on.

5. Mentor. We already discussed this, but I want to stress how important it is. You need to find someone in your industry who has accomplished *what you want to accomplish*. Get to know them and develop a relationship with them. These types of people can be key in offering guidance and industry-specific support. Additionally, your mentor should have contacts in the industry. They might help you find a new and better job if you're an employee. This is critical, as mentors can also help you with introductions to other successful people.

You should speak with all the members of your team once a quarter. Whether you need them or not, make a call to them every few months and give them a status update to keep your business or work life running smoothly. Keeping a few trusted advisors will put you in a good place if, and when, you need help, recommendations, and gritty advice.

ACTION STEPS: CONNECT WITH GAME FACERS

- **Make a list of Game Facers you know.** You don't have to know them personally yet, but make a list of people whom you want to get closer to.

- **Make the call.** Call your list of Game Facers and set up ten-minute appointments with them. It can be via phone or in person, but you want ten minutes of their time to ask for them to become your mentor.

- **Make a new connection today.** Start the process of building your team today. Is there someone you look up to or admire for their skills, their grit, or just for their sheer success? Good. Ask them for the name and number of their attorney, accountant, insurance agent, and banker. Then go so far as to ask them if you can take them to lunch once a quarter for mentoring advice.

CHAPTER 7

Step #4: Skill Up

GOING DEEP AND NARROW

I recently returned from a trip to Cuba. I was fortunate to get an inside view as Cuba reforms itself in the post-Castro regime. Cuba may be one of the most exciting stories of the next decade.

Located just ninety miles off the coast of the United States, it's like a time warp going fifty years into the past. Prior to the 1959 Castro revolution, Cuba was an extremely exciting country. In fact, in the late 1800s and early 1900s (1870–1910), Cuba was one of the wealthiest countries on the planet, primarily because of sugarcane. It's what created the opulent lifestyle and iconic art deco architecture that fills the country.

When you look at Cuba today, you see that opulence in despair, waiting to be rescued. Although Cuba still has some of the most gorgeous buildings you've ever seen, most are dilapidated and falling down. For entrepreneurs, this is a sight to behold. Entrepreneurs look at Cuba like a lion looks at raw meat. Somebody has to take advantage of the opportunities that have opened up there.

As Americans, we see the incredible upside. Americans think everyone wants what we want. But I met with Cuban entrepreneurs who assured me that this was not the case—they don't want the American lifestyle. They love their country, their culture—they even love their government. What they really want, from an entrepreneurial standpoint, is the Internet. They want to build their Lifestyle by Design, and to them, unlimited access to the Internet is the answer.

When we talked about how Americans use the Internet, the Cuban entrepreneurs laughed. They said, "Americans use the Internet *wide and shallow*. We want to use the Internet *deep and narrow*. We want to learn how to program video games, how to master the art of app building. We want the Internet in order to become masters of our own destiny."

We can all learn from this because they're right. We're busy sharing photos and watching cat videos, and Cubans want nothing to do with that; it's wasteful to them. Their limited access to the Internet focuses them to make the most of it.

We could learn a lesson from the Cubans about becoming specialized. We have become a society of *wide and shallow* where very few go *deep and narrow*. We want all of it at very low levels. That's why when it comes to money we never really make enough to make a difference in net worth. If you want to make more money, go deep and narrow. In other words, find a niche. Niches are hard to figure out because we're afraid that if we pick one niche, we limit ourselves or are protecting ourselves from making a wrong decision. But not picking a niche is the wrong decision.

WHY YOU NEED TO FIND YOUR NICHE

The business marketplace today is cloudy and crowded. For example: Got an idea to start a hamburger joint that serves cheap food fast? Try again. Want to serve gourmet coffee in a white cup with a logo and charge $5 a serving? Good luck.

Because so many business ideas and concepts are in place already, you need to work hard to find your niche. People in business who try to do everything for everyone don't make it anymore. Only deep and narrow works today. You need to have a niche in your life that separates you from the competition. Once you've found your niche, you need to market yourself as the expert in the niche so you can be noticed.

When I started my first business, I knew that there was money in the equipment finance industry. I realized very early on that large banks and finance companies loved financing new commercial fleet vehicles. At the time, I didn't understand the concept of finding my own niche, so I created my first company, Commercial Fleet Financing, Inc. (CFF), to focus on financing *new* commercial fleet vehicles. I was up against huge, publicly traded companies, and I didn't have a snowball's chance in hell.

After a few years of failing to gain traction and growth, I realized I needed to rethink my strategy in order to survive. I looked at my happiest clients, and my most profitable deals, and realized that they all had one thing in common: *used equipment*. The banks thought that low-level operators bought used because that was all they could afford, but the reality was that my best-credit customers bought only used equipment. Bingo. Opportunity just created itself. What the good-credit customers realized was that their customers didn't care whether the equipment was new and shiny or from a few years ago. Our customers knew what their customers wanted, and that was on-time delivery of product.

FIND A PROBLEM IN YOUR INDUSTRY TO SOLVE

Where do you go looking for your niche? The best way to distinguish yourself and gain traction toward success is to help to *solve a problem in your industry*. Once you've used the Litmus Test to pick the platform that will help you achieve your Lifestyle by Design, you need to identify the most pressing problems affecting that industry. Some of these will be bigger than others, but they all have opportunities to be solved by someone, and that someone can get rich doing it. The idea is to find your niche by identifying the right problem and creating a solution to solve it.

I found my niche by understanding a big problem in the transportation industry, which led me to build the company that got me out of Broke and into Rich. Here's how I did it.

Shortly after I started CFF, the price of new equipment began to escalate, but the economics of the business was slow to catch up. Let's use a typical example: We love to finance tow trucks. Small or large, we love them all. At CFF, we believe that as the population grows, more cars (whether gas or electric or self-driving) will hit the roads. More cars will create more break-downs and accidents, so a tow truck will always be needed in the marketplace. Therefore, the financing of tow trucks will always be needed. We observed that even if a tow truck that used to cost $50,000 now costs $100,000, the towing company wouldn't be able to double their prices. So we solved the problem by special-izing in used equipment to allow our towing customers to main-tain their profitability without doubling their prices. It played right into our hands. With a little research and analysis of a problem, we identified and occupied a new niche in the market.

When it became clear to me that my competition—large, publicly traded banks—didn't want to finance used equipment, in that moment, my narrow niche was born. I decided CFF would be the best used-equipment financing company on the planet. Although we still finance new equipment, CFF is now known as a leader in used-equipment financing. Understanding our niche, and marketing ourselves as the expert in this niche, saved my business. You need to find the same type of niche for your business.

The key to winning business in a niche market is twofold:

1. **Become an expert in your niche.** To become an expert, skill up (we'll get into this in the next chapter) and cover all of your

bases in your chosen niche. This may require additional licenses, bonds, certifications, ratings, and background checks. Customers will pay for expertise, but you have to do the work first, because they can see a phony coming from a mile away. It's worth it to do the work, because as an expert, you can charge more and will be paid more. **Remember: Amateurs get crushed and experts get paid. Make sure you're choosing a niche based on skills you have or can attain.**

2. **Market yourself as the expert.** It's not enough to just be an expert in your niche. You need to own it, and market yourself as an expert. Everything you do, from your business cards, e-mail signature lines, media materials, brochures, Web sites, social media, and even the sign on your door, must tell the marketplace that you are an expert. The best customers are not looking for what you are selling—they are looking for your expertise.

To find your niche, ask yourself these questions:

- What's an unsolved problem or an underserved market in my industry?
- Why do my best customers do business with me?
- What are my competitors *not* doing that I *can* do?
- Can I be *better* than the current players?
- Is this niche a flash in the pan or a long-term career or business?

Pick a niche, market yourself as the expert in this niche, and continue to look for new opportunities within the niche.

MONEY FOLLOWS SKILLS AND SKILLS ARE YOUR RESPONSIBILITY

So let's say you've identified a problem in your industry that you want to solve, and have decided to go deep and narrow on it. How do you develop the skills to do it? Contrary to popular belief, if you are employed by a company, that company has no responsibility to develop your skills. I'm constantly asked by new people who come to apply for a position with my company, "What sort of training do you offer?"

The answer is always the same: I'm not in the training business. I'm in the equipment financing business. My job is not to hire you and then train you. My job is to hire highly skilled equipment financing pros with an existing book of business who like my company culture and my compensation plan more than that of their current employer. The goal is to provide an opportunity that allows people with desire, smarts, and ambition to thrive. In order to accomplish this, I do provide extensive sales training via the best sales training program on the planet, Cardone University, and a video-based sales training manual on how my business and industry works. Between our company videos and our YouTube channel, we have more than one thousand videos that cover just about any subject in my industry you could imagine. But anyone in my business will have to put in the work. I don't pay people to watch videos, read books, and get motivated— I pay people to produce. If you get hired, you get all the tools to make you successful (we pay tens of thousands of dollars a year for these tools), but it is your responsibility to use them and skill yourself up. As my friend Brad Lea, founder of Lightspeed VT, says best, "I can save you from drowning, but you have to swim to me."

Understand that your employer is paying you to bring your *value* to the company—not your *lack* of skills—so it's your job, not your employer's, to make sure you are skilled up.

Recently, I walked by Lucy, one of the receptionists at my company, leaning back in her chair, looking at her Facebook account when I walked by.

I asked her, "Are you busy?"

She said, "Not right now, I'm just waiting for the phone to ring." Wrong answer.

I stopped what I was doing and asked her to come to my office for a little talk.

Lucy was a single mother who needed more. More time, more freedom, more skills, and damn sure more money. She knew it and so did I. But despite knowing this, she just wasn't pushing herself to bring more value. She and everyone around her knew that she was falling behind, at work and financially, but she couldn't find a way to take action and make a change. You may be a single mom who needs more money, and you know it, too. Everyone around you knows it, including your friends and your children. Deep down, late at night, you know you have more to give, but you just haven't made the connection yet between working and adding value. Added value is your insurance policy. When you do something better than anyone else in your company or your industry, you will make more money. But if you're waiting for someone else to make it happen for you, I want you to know that no one has that responsibility. It's up to you.

If you have a job in which you have downtime, you have the perfect opportunity to skill up. Someone else is paying you to learn! But perhaps you think someone else is paying you for your hours or your time, and therefore you're just milking the clock. That's the worst possible attitude you could have. It's the complete opposite of what you should think. You should be thinking, *How did I get so lucky to be a receptionist who has enough free time in the day that I can get paid to develop my skills?*

I asked Lucy to commit to me that she would use any downtime she had to skill up. She agreed and followed my advice. From that moment on, whenever she had downtime, I would see her walking around the office asking people if she could shadow them. She would ask people in various departments, "Could you show me how you do that?" and our team would happily oblige. She quickly came to understand our business and successfully transferred into our operations department—at a pay scale 50 percent higher than that of a receptionist.

Whether you're a receptionist or a general manager, it's time for you to get to work at skilling up. You know what you're good at, so why not skill up and get to the next level? Sure, it's good to learn about every aspect of your business and industry, but only to help you become better at your job, in your niche.

It's obvious that the best in every industry make the most money. So don't worry about what you suck at. Worry about maxing out your superpower. Working on improving your weaknesses has limited value. I suggest you find what you already do well, and focus your attention on turning that skill into your superpower. By working on what you're good at, you have the potential to become extraordinary.

Every industry is a great industry for the top 1 percent. If you're in the top 1 percent of all garbagemen in the world, you're making a ton of cash. Most people think that being a garbageman is a bad business, but they're wrong. Being in the top 1 percent of *any* industry is how to get paid. Sure, it might be harder to get to the top 1 percent in an industry that is saturated, like the coffee shop business, and you should pick a platform in which many people can find success, but the best of the best is always going to dominate, regardless.

The problem is that most people never strive to get to the top 1 percent. They may start in the bottom 99 percent and work their way up to the middle 50 percent. This is where the bills get paid, so they stop skilling up. Ask yourself:

- Who are you reading, who are you listening to, who are you watching?
- How much time do you spend on learning, as opposed to on mind-numbing activities?

The higher your skill level, the more dramatically your money situation will improve.

WHAT'S YOUR SUPERPOWER?

I want you to sit down with the five Game Facers whose opinion you value. You're going to ask them (and yourself—that's right, write down your own answers) big questions to help you understand what you're good at, and therefore what business you should be in. Bonus points if they are financially where you want to be. Allowing yourself to be open to feedback from your friends, family, coworkers, and even perfect strangers is *vital* to understanding where you are currently.

In each of these conversations, ask:

- What do they (and you) see as your strengths and weaknesses?
- What kinds of skills are you great at?
- What industry or career path do they see you thriving in?
- What kinds of questions or problems would they come to you with?
- What expertise of yours do they value?
- What do they think you do at an exceptional level?

GETTING BETTER AT YOUR SUPERPOWER

It has never been easier to develop your skills. You can learn anything you want for free. It's called YouTube! If I had walked by my receptionist and she'd been on YouTube watching videos about truckers so she'd have something to talk to clients about when they call on the phone, I'd applaud her effort in skilling up! Hell, if she was on YouTube learning how to play piano I would have been excited for her! I would have said, "Good for you, and shame on me for not keeping you busier!"

So, what are some of the ways you can skill up? Here is my five-step program:

1. What do you like?

Don't start with learning things that you don't like. The key here is to develop the desire to become a master at just a few things so that you have the confidence to become a master all of your life, and you won't stick with something long enough to achieve mastery unless you enjoy it. Lifelong learners lead interesting lives and develop mastery that lets them make the most money.

2. What value can you bring to the organization at all times?

Ask yourself: What is your company *not* doing that you think it should be doing? How can you fill your time with activity that helps the company fill in this gap? This puts you in the driver's seat. If you become the in-house expert on how to do what your company is not doing, you become *much* more valuable, and then you can leverage that value for a pay raise.

3. No white space on your calendar

If your workday opens with white space, giving you lots of downtime, you need to fill in those gaps on your calendar with learning opportunities.

Think of it like this: If you're feeling sick and you call your doctor and your doctor says, "We have no appointments today. Choose whenever you'd like to come in," then you should probably find a different doctor. When you fill up your calendar you will radically change your income situation because some of the wealthiest people I know are also the busiest people I know. I'm not talking about creating busywork for yourself. I'm talking about making sure you are using every minute of every day to get closer to your Lifestyle by Design. Scheduling meetings with mentors, learning new skills, selling more product, even spending quiet time visualizing your success and Lifestyle by Design—it all goes into filling up your calendar and it's all important to helping you make more money.

As Mark Cuban said, "When I became a billionaire, I thought I would have more free time. The reality is, I've never been busier."

Whether you use a physical calendar, Google calendar, or Outlook, just start filling in those blank spaces.

4. Every skill has inherent value

If you learn to play piano, that can make you better at business. How? Because piano or guitar or flute is a new language. And learning new languages opens up new doors in your brain for communication. So, if you're in business, but you teach yourself how to play piano, I bet you'll be a better communicator. I know for damn sure that you'll be more interesting at the next Christmas party—among all your other responsibilities you've learned to play piano and can bust out some Billy Joel "Piano Man." Keep learning and doing the things you love, besides learning the specific skills you need to advance at work. These not only make your life better, but you never know how they may help you at your current job and open up opportunities to make more money. And it also makes you more interesting, which brings me to my next point . . .

5. Become a person of interest

> Interesting people do interesting things.
>
> —Jim Rohn

I love this quote from Jim Rohn because it's 100 percent true. Learn to do something that makes you interesting. Why? You'll find that the easiest way to open doors, make connections, and have opportunities come to you is to be interesting. When you're introduced to people you want to meet, you'll want to have more to talk about than how business is going.

Being a person of interest is easy:

1. **Do stuff that is interesting to you.** Complete a triathlon. Volunteer to coach or mentor kids in your community. Ride a bike across the country. Play Rachmaninoff's Concerto no. 3 on the piano. Write a book. Do whatever floats your boat, but do something cool and interesting and different.

2. **Have a bio.** You need a quick one-paragraph to one-page bio of yourself that highlights your unique attributes. Where you grew up, your career story, your superpower, and some of the interesting things you have done should all be in it. If you're having trouble writing about yourself, just get someone to write your bio for you. An easy place to get this done is www .fiverr.com. For $5–$10, you can find someone who will write it for you. Just send them the bullet points of what makes you interesting and they will write a beautiful bio about you.

3. **Get your bio seen online.** When someone types your name into Google, they need to find something. Something about YOU must pop up, and the more they can find, the better. It has never been easier to control this result. The search engine "bots" (computer programs designed to find relevant search results)—as they are called for Google, Bing, Yahoo!, etc.— crave content, so give it to them and put your best foot forward. One of the best and easiest ways to make this happen

is by simply posting your bio to LinkedIn. It takes one minute. In short order it will be found by search engines and it will start showing up anytime someone types your name into Google.

THE POWER OF NIGHTS AND WEEKENDS

The workday is for you to be doing whatever it is you do to earn a living. You are doing what you have to do to keep your job, or if you are in business for yourself, to guide and support your people, make calls, lead meetings, sell your product or service, and pay your bills. Most competent people can get through this part just fine. What separates the experts from the amateurs is how you spend your nights and weekends. While your pals are all cutting out at 5 p.m. and binge-watching Netflix, you need to be doing the exact opposite. Nights and weekends are your time to *pounce*. It's your time to get ahead. To learn, to prepare, and to make more money. **Nights and weekends are for massive focus—focus that separates you from the others. It is the time for you to do what others *won't* do.**

I tell new salespeople in my office that it is mathematically impossible for them to work as many Saturdays and Sundays as I have because I have worked so many weekends over the past twenty-two years that even if they worked every day until the end of their career, they still wouldn't catch up to me. I already have and will continue to work more Saturdays and Sundays.

I'm interested in getting ahead in life. I don't want average or normal or middle of the road. I spent way too much of my life thinking that way. I want more, and I want the same for you. The ability to put in the extra time to watch, listen, learn, read, and think is the reason why successful people are successful. People who put in the minimum effort from nine to five don't get ahead. They sit in the parking lot for one last smoke and open the door to the office with no time to spare. They leave for lunch right at noon and return just before 1:00 p.m. They start packing up their desk at 4:30 so they can hit the exit when the clock strikes 5:00. Fridays are the start of the weekend for them. What a joke! Don't be surprised when doing the bare minimum gets you the bare minimum.

What happens on nights and weekends makes the difference between the winners and the losers in the game of finances, and here's why. My customers are working during the day, so they don't want to take a sales call during that time. However, they are available to take a 7:00 p.m. sales call. They'll take my call at 7:00 a.m. or 9:00 a.m. on a Saturday or 8:30 a.m. before church on a Sunday. Early mornings, evenings, and weekends are not just important in communicating with a client, but they're also important in strategizing your individual plan.

ACTION STEPS: MAKE BETTER USE OF YOUR TIME

Late nights and weekends are for preparation and skilling up. As I said before, it is not your employer's responsibility to help you skill up. If you are lucky enough to work for an employer who pays for your schooling or on-the-job training, congratulations. Jump on that benefit. But no matter who pays for it, *you* still need to put in the extra time to skill up. Here are my suggestions on how to use late nights and weekends to make more money:

1. **Make more sales calls.** Some people feel hesitant about making calls before or after business hours, but the calls you make during these off-hours can be the most effective. Getting on the phone earlier and later will help you get in touch with that prospect who is too busy during the normal day to speak to you. Another added benefit to making these calls outside normal working hours is that you bypass the gatekeeper. The executive assistant who has been blocking you from the CEO isn't there at 7:00 a.m. or 7:00 p.m. That creates opportunity for you to make a direct impression on the person you want to do business with. Make the most important calls when your chances of getting through cleanly are maximized.

2. **Get organized.** We all spend so much time getting caught up in the day-to-day of whatever it is we do. Most of the time we are wrapped up in reaction mode, answering e-mails, responding to crises, and putting out fires. Late nights and weekends help us organize our activities and focus on doing meaningful, impactful work, which is what ultimately makes us more money.

3. **Make connections.** Invite people to coffee or lunch to get to know them better. Use late nights and weekends as a time to

get your personal brand popping on social media and connect to influencers by liking and sharing their content.

4. **Get better at your superpower.** This bears repeating again here. Watch videos, read books, and practice to increase your skills. Who is already great at what you can be great at? What do they do? How do they do it? Are there tools they use or created that can help you?

5. **Just think.** Our days tend to get so busy that they don't leave us with much time to just pull back and think. Use late nights and weekends to also just put your feet up and dream. These quiet moments are great moments for this type of thinking. I'm often caught up in running my business, but for many years now, I've made it a practice to take five to ten minutes out of my day to close the door to my office, sit in my chair, put my feet up, and stare at the ceiling. That's my quiet time and it lowers my blood pressure. This is usually the time when I'm able to see the answer to a problem I've been trying to solve instead of constantly pushing against a rock. Sometimes you have to take a step back from the frantic pace of your day to be able to see the forest for the trees.

6. **Fill the calendar.** I need to make a point of taking time out of my day to think, because I fill the rest of my day with structured and productive activities. Chances are you that you have way too much free time you could be using to make more money. If you actually pull out your calendar and fill in your time slots, you will quickly see how much free time you actually have. You need only six to eight hours of sleep per

night. That leaves sixteen to eighteen hours per day to get busy. Not just a little busy, I'm talking about filling the calendar up.

7. **Set your goals again and often.** Goals matter. It's tough to set goals once you're in the middle of a busy workday, so you need to dedicate time outside your workday to focus on goal setting. Take some time on Sunday night to set your goals for the week. Come in early every morning before work to set your daily goals before the e-mails start coming in. Write your goals down on paper and keep them in front of your face at all times. Use the time during your nights and weekends to stay laser-focused on achieving them.

CHAPTER 8

Step #5: Time for a Raise: How to Get More Money from Your Current Job

MORE VALUE EQUALS A RAISE

If you're working for an employer, right now, you're either more valuable to your company than you're getting paid for, or you should be looking to bring more value so that you deserve to get paid more. It's time for a raise. Even if you've decided that you want to quit and create your own business (which we'll get into in the next chapter), you're not going to (and shouldn't) quit your job cold turkey. So it's still important to learn how to maximize your moneymaking at your primary job until you can get things going.

When it comes to creating value, you have an advantage over your boss and other higher-ups. You are the one on the front lines, and the front lines are where the action is. You know the problems in your department. You see them before

173

your boss does, and often more clearly. This gives you an opportunity to be a proactive problem solver. Act as if you have an antenna on your head, constantly looking for problems. Key point here: You are not looking for problems to whine about. You are looking for problems that you can solve. You are now a professional problem solver, and in quick order you will start to earn more money.

Take this example from General Electric (GE). In the 1950s, GE created Crotonville on a gorgeous mountaintop about an hour's drive north of New York City. Crotonville is where GE brings their best and brightest to train and get better. It has long been considered GE's "secret weapon." During one of the working sessions at Crotonville, a factory worker for GE was in the audience. As management presented the complex problem of the day, all the top brass worked back and forth on the whiteboard. They dissected the problem and attempted to find solutions for an issue within one of their manufacturing plants, but couldn't make much headway. Finally, near the end of the session, the factory worker raised his hand and said, "You guys don't know what you are talking about. I deal with this problem every day. Let me show you how to fix this." With that, he went to the whiteboard and, within minutes, he outlined the solution that the top brass couldn't figure out. He knew the problem backward and forward because he had to deal with it every day. Because of this, he also knew how to solve the problem and was ready with the solution.

You have that same power. Don't wait for your higher-ups to

fix anything. Screw the organizational chart, the traditional hierarchy. The quickest way to get noticed in your organization is to identify and solve problems, and problem solvers always get paid more than people who just ignore or gripe about their problems.

Be on the lookout for unique problems. If something within your department is broken, be the fixer. Create a plan to solve this problem. Create a presentation that outlines this problem, the reason the problem should be solved, and the expected outcome once it is solved. Then ask for a meeting with your boss to present your findings and your solution. This presentation should be done with the utmost professionalism. It could be one of the biggest presentations of your life, so don't take it lightly. Do your research and analysis and knock it out of the park. Have booklets, or PowerPoints, or graphs or testimonials or data, whatever you need, to show that you have taken the time to figure it out. Then dress for success and present it. An important note here: Make your boss look good. You might even need to allow your boss to take the credit for it. But you and she will know whose idea it was, and you can leverage that in the very near future when you ask for your raise.

GETTING RECOGNIZED FOR YOUR WORTH

Whether you've decided you're better off as an employee or employer based on your Lifestyle by Design, the foundational principles of success are the same either way:

1. **You need to prove your value to the marketplace at all times.** You must do more than is expected of you from either your boss or your clients. If you do this consistently, your income will grow, and if you don't, you will get your ass handed to you.

2. **You must sell yourself.** You make your own breaks. Don't wait. Push for opportunities at all times. You might think that this will rub your boss the wrong way. Too bad. You are in charge of you, and self-promotion is important. Hell, if you don't promote yourself, why would you expect anyone else to promote you? Feel good about yourself, and sell the hell out of yourself every chance you get. The squeaky wheel does get the grease.

3. **Don't assume . . . ask.** Never make the assumption that your boss or your clients know what you want—they don't. You know what they want? What THEY want! Not what you want! They are not thinking of you. They are thinking of themselves. So, don't assume that your raise or that new batch of business will come to you from them. You must ask for it and you must ask for it often.

4. **Be ready or don't ask.** Are you ready for the next level or are you just a pain in my neck? If you come to me for a raise, you better be prepared. Have your act together, and be like a rocket ship ready to blast off. If you come to me dressed sloppily, without a presentation that includes data and support of your request, you will not get what you want. Getting to the next level financially requires you to play at an entirely new level.

GET PAID TODAY

My inability to understand how to value my services, communicate my value, and actually move the needle of my net worth plagued me during the early years of my business. Don't let it happen to you. **You must get paid for your services. The reality is that very rarely will people *want* to pay you what you are worth—that is just a fact of business.** Once again, that is not the fault of the marketplace. It is YOUR fault. If you don't get paid properly, that is your issue, just as it was mine. But you can quickly fix this situation and consistently get paid what you deserve and more by doing these things:

- **Research:** Understand the market and the pricing structure of competitors. You might also need to do a cost/benefit analysis if you're selling a physical product that takes a certain amount of money and time to create. Now you have an idea of what you need to charge, either for services (like hourly or per project) or for the product.
- **Negotiate:** If you're in a situation where the price is negotiable, really push for your worth. Speak up—don't just let the other side bully you and get what they want. Know going in what your minimum is and what you're willing to give in on. Maybe you're willing to take a lower price to work with a special client because they're a charity or can create other opportunities for you—factor in all of that when you negotiate.

- **Payment terms:** Make sure you don't complete a deal without fully understanding the payment structure. Do you get paid 50 percent up front and 50 percent when the job is done? Is it a weekly payment schedule? How many days do they have to pay you? Will they be penalized if they pay you late?
- **Know before you go:** Make sure all of this is decided before you start work. Do the research and analysis. You don't want any surprises on game day!

The point is to recognize this epidemic of not getting paid what you're worth and to *do something about it.*

PROVE YOUR VALUE

As an employer of people within a $100 million–plus business, I am focused on growth at all times. Because of my focus, at times I neglect the compensation of people within my organization. I wish it was different and that I was alone in this, but it is not, and I am not. At the end of the day, I'm interested in building a great company that is indestructible because of the business practices we have and the amount of cash we have stuffed in the coffers. That is my job. Your job is to make me notice you. It is also to make sure that I pay you what you are worth. That is not my job, it is *yours.*

Here's what I mean: I hired Jason, a twenty-two-year-old kid with no college background and virtually no business experience at all, but I saw something within him during the interview process. This kid had a great, can-do attitude. He wanted a shot, someone to believe in him and show him the ropes. He reminded me of myself in a way. We needed someone in our documentation department, so I offered him that job. The pay was $30,000 and he could take it or leave it. He took it and never negotiated for one dollar more. This turned out to be a smart move on his part because I thought I got a good deal, and he realized that he could only go up.

Jason would prepare the loan documents for customers to sign and when deal flow was slow, Jason would come into my office and ask, "What is the biggest problem I can help you with this week, boss? Anything. Throw it at me and let me do my best to solve it for you."

At first I would give him small tasks that I couldn't care less about.

"Go organize the storage closet," I would say.

He would say, with an ear-to-ear smile, "It shall be done, boss."

And sure as shit, when his department was slow, he would go into that storage closet and start organizing, cleaning, and tossing the junk. He would spend about thirty minutes each day doing this side job, and when it was done, he swung by my office to let me know it was done and asked me to inspect it for my approval. His work was good, both as a documentation specialist and as storage room organizer. He immediately asked for another project, and I found something to give him. He would always have an extra side project in the works with me, something above and beyond his primary job. He simply took care of things that needed to be done at a level that required little supervision and didn't distract him or anyone else from their primary job.

So when he asked for a raise, it was a no-brainer for both of us. He quickly started earning another couple dollars per hour. Peanuts for me, but to him it was a significant raise. This process of Jason asking to "help solve my problems" happened almost weekly. Soon I wasn't giving him any direction. He was identifying and solving problems I didn't even realize existed. He was taking the bull by the horns and just getting it done.

He brought me a new version of our company newsletter, which was so good I approved it immediately.

He arranged for me to be interviewed by a major trade magazine, a great opportunity to promote our business.

He started promoting our financing specials on all of our social media platforms, as well as engaging with prospective clients who wanted to buy equipment, which I found truly impressive.

It was all well done and it exceeded my expectations. Sure as hell, sixty days later, he came into my office and told me that our newsletter and the social media effort had generated eight new deals for us. Our average deal size is $50,000, so his little newsletter project had generated $400,000 worth of new business for us.

I will never forget what he said: "What a great idea you had, boss. This newsletter was really a hit. I'm so glad you gave me the opportunity to carry out your idea and generate us $400,000 worth of new deals."

This kid was smooth. So smooth that he got another raise. After about six months with us, he was earning $36,000 per year, which was a $6,000—or 20 percent—raise in six months, and all because he asked for responsibility, got it, did the work above expectations, and reminded me of the value that his work brought to the company.

Shortly after the success of his newsletter, he took over our social media efforts, without my asking him to. Next thing I knew, we had our Twitter, Facebook, Instagram, and LinkedIn popping. I bet you can guess what happened next . . . into my office came Jason, with reports of the social media success stories we had. Before his one-year anniversary, Jason was earning $48,000, which was $18,000 over his starting salary! In a world where many people get 3 percent annual raises from their employer, Jason had earned a 60 percent raise because of a great attitude, asking for more responsibility, proving that he brought value to the organization, and then leveraging it by asking for a raise.

By the end of year two, he had continued to find ways to provide more value without anyone asking him to. He was so ahead of me and so in charge of his movement and future that I wasn't able to keep up with him. So many employees move slower than management, just following orders and waiting for more instruction, but not Jason. He was always a step ahead, creating value for us and value for him because of his pace. At the end of his second year, he had taken charge of our marketing efforts and was earning $65,000 per year. Think about that: Within two years, he had earned $35,000 more than when he started. At twenty-four, with no college degree or prior business experience, he was earning $65,000 and earning more than his father. If you do the math on this, his annual raises were over 50 percent EACH YEAR!

Although Jason's efforts were paying for themselves, he reached his compensation cap—$65,000 was the top of the pay scale for his position within my company. When I mentioned this to him during his last raise discussion, he said he understood. Thirty days later, he put in his resignation. He thanked me for the amazing opportunity I'd provided him, but he wanted to continue his income-earning path and he had accepted a marketing job at another company for $75,000 per year. Last I heard, he was earning $150,000 as the head of marketing for a small tech company—all this before he turned thirty. That's the power of attitude, gratitude, asking for responsibility, creating value, exceeding expectations, and leveraging it all for more money.

Jason had a knack for making sure that I was made aware of the value he brought to me and my company. It was like clockwork every sixty days: he would request a meeting with me to discuss his compensation and leave my office with a raise. Why give it to him? At each meeting he showed me the value he was bringing to my company and proving his indisputable worth to me.

It's not that hard to do what Jason did, and dramatically ramp up your earning. All you have to do is commit now to putting in focus and effort to finding new value inside of your career.

Stop waiting for someone to tell you to solve problems and just start solving them. He did what you need to do: you need to understand what value you bring to the organization, bring it at a level that is exceptional (far above what is expected), and then leverage it for more money.

One last point: when it comes to producing exceptional value . . . keep it real at all times. I get such a kick out of seeing the amount of BS people feed their brains. So many of us compare our successes downward, looking at the success or failure of someone who has not achieved what we want to achieve and using that as our goal line. This process allows us to feel good about ourselves because we did better than a loser. It is the exact opposite of what we need to do. Never compare yourself down— always compare yourself up.

MULTIPLY YOUR VALUE WITH SOCIAL MEDIA

The Internet and social media are filled with posers, phonies, and fakes, but that is not you. By now you know your strengths; you have taken one or two of them and turned it into a superpower. Now you have the makings of an exceptional and interesting personal brand. It's time to get it out there.

If you don't have a personal brand, regardless of whether you're the employer or the employee, in today's marketplace you are costing yourself, your family, and your organization money. The reason is that a personal brand helps bring value to your company. I am not talking about just having and running Twitter and

Facebook pages because you feel like you have to. I am talking about using this to your advantage in a concrete way. Think about it like this: If you solve a problem for your boss, or develop expertise in a new field, you only create value for your boss and your company. But if you then also share your solution or your expertise on social media, you create value for hundreds, maybe thousands, of others. This helps get you noticed as a problem solver and helps you move up and make more money. You are far more valuable with an audience because an audience amplifies your value and travels with you, and you can end up getting paid more because of that audience. I fought against this idea for way too long in my career, thinking the way to get ahead was by just putting my head down and quietly doing the work. Now I realize how much money it cost me.

At my company, we have a "CFF Morning Scrum" every day. It is a ten-minute all-staff meeting in which we discuss the successes of the previous day and what we are working on for today. We often play a quick motivational video to get the group fired up as well. During one of our morning scrums in 2013, I made a now infamous statement to my entire company: "Mark my words: social media will go down as the biggest waste of time in the history of business."

Boy, was I wrong. I looked at social media (and everything at that time) in terms of return on investment (ROI), completely missing the two most important reasons of why social media is so important:

Number 1: It's FREE. Facebook, Twitter, LinkedIn, Snapchat, Instagram, and YouTube cost nothing. *Zero.* In the old days, if you wanted to build a brand—to be seen and to attract and build an audience—you had to take out radio ads, television commercials, or maybe even billboards on the highway. The cost was immense and prohibitive for most people and small businesses. Today, you can create an account on any of these platforms in about two minutes.

Number 2: Your story. Everyone has a story and there is an audience for every story. People are attracted to your business when they know your story. The marketplace loves stories. The rags-to-riches story, the hero's-journey story, the triumph-over-evil story. However you frame your own story, stories are interesting and valuable, and far more effective than mission statements or empty promises. Your clients, your coworkers, and your industry want to hear and see your story. With social media, it's never been easier to tell it.

By simply being active on social media and sharing your experiences of work and your industry, you become a well-known, credible expert in your space. Sure, you're an expert already because you've worked at becoming the best in your niche, but does anyone know that? Not if you don't start sharing your expertise with an audience. Don't get stuck in the old mentality, that social is about personal use only. Sure, a lot of people have made money without it, but they are part of the old guard. Having a social media presence is becoming increasingly important in a variety of industries, if not essential. Think about how many people will Google you before pulling the trigger on doing business with you. Social media is to be used to make you stand out as an expert in your industry, and here's how you do it:

1. **Create pages on all social media platforms.** *All* platforms. You need a Facebook page, Twitter page, Instagram page, YouTube page, LinkedIn page, and Snapchat account. Some people might tell you to focus on just a couple platforms, but I say you need a strong presence on all of them. Hey, it's what those late nights and weekends are for. But if you really can't deal with all those platforms? Then focus on LinkedIn, YouTube, and Facebook.

2. **Like, comment, and share content.** You may not be ready to generate and create your own content, and that is okay for now. You will eventually need to create content to fully build a personal brand, but to get started, you can simply like, comment, and share other people's content. Share videos that relate to your industry. If you drive a truck for a living, post cool pictures of trucks. Share articles that relate to the trucking industry. Use other people's content to help position you as someone who knows the industry. But a word of caution: As someone who puts out a ton of original content, nothing pisses me off more than when someone takes my content and passes it off as their own. Simply give credit where credit is due and link back

to the source, because nothing makes me like you more on social media than when you share my content and say nice things about me. Do the same for influencers within your industry. This helps you get attention from them, and when you start to generate your own content, they will return the favor.

3. **Hit record.** Recording videos are the best way to create content, build an audience, and max out your personal brand. You might not believe it, but everyone is interested in your expertise, so hit record. You've got a camera right on your phone. Do what my coach and friend Hank Norman says to do: "Show me you doing what you do best."

Let me give you a real-life example of how your personal brand can make you more valuable and then make you more money: I have a friend, Victoria, in the apartment leasing business. Right out of school, she started working the front office of a large apartment complex and her job was to lease out one-, two-, or three-bedroom apartments. Victoria was always friendly to prospective clients and continued that friendliness online—she created social media pages to reach out online to anyone who came into her building and she began to create a following. This became her "tribe," as author Seth Godin calls it.

She started to make videos, taking her online audience on a tour of the one-bedroom with granite countertops and wall-to-wall carpet, or the five-bedroom penthouse apartment with a view of the city skyline. She would take her audience on a tour of the pool in the apartment complex, and the attached clubhouse gym. Victoria drew an audience because she wasn't just showing apartments—she was showing a lifestyle people could visualize themselves in.

When people were ready to move, they would think of her first. Because of the personal brand she'd built, people often felt a connection to Victoria and trusted her even before they met her. People didn't just reach out to her more often, they were eager to close a deal with her quickly. In this way, she brought value to her apartment complex and her employer and put more money in her pocket along the way with more commissions. But that's not all.

Victoria noticed a new apartment complex being built right around the corner. She saw that the new complex was better, with more amenities, and she quickly realized that they would be a formidable competitor to her complex. She knew they would need leasing agents, so she interviewed with them for a new job.

During that interview, Victoria showed the owner her content and social media following, along with all her expertise in the apartment leasing industry. The owner was immediately able to see the incredible value Victoria brought in connecting with prospective leasers and closing deals quickly, and hired her on the spot. Victoria is now one of the top leasing agents in her town.

Think about it: Would your new potential employer hire someone who says they'll do a good job, or would they prefer to hire someone who can show them proof of it, through their video content and built-in audience? Of course employers want the candidate with a personal brand. You bring automatic customers with you and you will be hired over someone who doesn't bring in business. Bingo. You just brought more value than the next applicant and you can charge more for your value. Period, end of story.

GET A RAISE IN A WEEK

All right, let's get real: this is my foolproof method for how to get a raise as an employee within one week of doing what I explain in this section. Think about the power in that statement: *you* are going to get yourself a raise. But first, you need to make sure you deserve one.

Because you are in charge, you are also now the Chief Marketing Officer of yourself. This is a phrase my friend Bethany Williams, author of the book *3 Days to a Raise* uses often. Bethany says—and I agree fully—that "people need, in every position, within every company, to be the Chief Marketing Officer of *them*!" Time to become the CMO of you to get a raise—time to market and sell yourself. How? Here is what Bethany and I suggest (and you've got a week to do it all):

1. **Know your value.** Go on www.salary.com or www.glassdoor .com and see what the market is paying for a position similar to the one you currently hold. What is the annual salary or the going hourly rate being paid for your position? Pull the salary ranges and see where you stand.

2. **Build ammo.** You need to keep a folder—either digital or hard copy—of everything you have done and achieved. Did you win salesperson of the month? Great, print out the results showing you at the top. Have your customers left you a review on Google or Facebook and mentioned your name specifically? Great, screenshot it and put it in your folder. Just as important as it is to solve problems and add value, you need to be sure you're tracking that value. Remember Jason, who showed me that he generated $400,000 in sales from his newsletter? I couldn't argue with those hard results.

3. **Know your numbers.** What are your sales? How much business have *you* generated? How much have you saved or made for the company because of the ideas you created and executed on? Have your information ready *before* you walk into your boss's office.

4. **Collect testimonials.** Your best customers or coworkers, *if* you have done exceptional work and produced exceptional results, will write you a testimonial. This could be on paper or on Yelp, Google, or Facebook. Wherever they posted it, you want it because it will be part of your annual report. Which brings me to . . .

5. **Create an annual report.** This is not the time for verbal-only communication. Nobody on Wall Street takes the CFO's word for the results of their company. CFOs create an annual report and you should, too. The annual report is simply a presentation of the results you've had over the past year. Create your annual report as a PowerPoint or handout. It should

include a summary of your results, highlights of all your successes, and the value you have brought to the company. Don't go light here. Put your best foot forward.

6. **Know how much you want.** Now that you know your money gap, your value, what your position pays at other companies, and how much value you have brought to your employer, you need to know how much to ask for. *Do not leave it up to your boss.* And don't buy into the BS from human resources when you hear, "We can only give 3 percent raises." Ask for how much you want.

It doesn't matter if you are the employee or the employer—you need to view yourself as your own business. This means understanding the problem you solve, understanding the value you bring to solving the problem, and—key point—*understanding that regardless of the position you hold, you must connect it to revenue generation.* Everyone, in every organization, is their own salesperson.

MOVE UP OR MOVE OUT

What if you followed my plan and you *still* don't get a raise? You will need to go back and reread the last chapter, skill up, and bring more value to the situation. Once you do, present again. If you do this and still do not get a raise, then do what my friend Andrea did, and prepare to leave. You have to get paid your value.

My friend Andrea would come through Dallas a few times each year for work. She is in the fashion business, and four times per year Dallas has a large apparel mart in which designers and manufacturers present their seasonal products. When I was in the beginning stages of starting my company, I was straight broke all the time. So I loved when Andrea would roll through Dallas because she found me to be good company and would extend an invitation to me when she was entertaining clients on her corporate account. But every few months, as she came to present her products at the mart, she was always with a new company.

When I asked her why, she always said the new company paid her more. She was never afraid to leave her current employer for more money and is now a top executive for a New York City fashion company. She understood her value. She had the confidence to always overdeliver and was never afraid to remind her superiors of the quality of work that she did. Value deserves payment, especially for those who have the guts and who are willing to ask for it. Andrea, every six months, would go into her boss's office and remind them of the value she brought to the company and ask for a raise. When they agreed with her and gave her a raise, she stayed. When they agreed with her and didn't give her a raise, for whatever the reason—budget issues, whatever the hocus-pocus the company created for not paying her for the value she brought—she left. She would go to another employer and get paid what she deserved.

If you're growing meteorically, there may come a point when you outgrow your company. The more of an expert you are, the more value you create, and you might find the rest of your company can't keep up with you.

Each and every time, I saw Andrea repeat this process:

- Skill up
- Commit to being the best
- Bring value far above the job description and expectations
- Go in to ask the boss for a raise every few months
- Get the raise

Or . . .

You might have to leave your job if you're not getting paid your value, but never leave your job without having another one lined up. Or, better yet, create a job for yourself and be your own Personal ATM. How? That's what we'll get into in the next chapter.

ACTION STEPS: KNOW YOUR VALUE

- **Research your comparable salary today.** Find out how much other companies are paying people in your position.
- **How are you valuable?** Write down all the ways in which you've created value for your organization in the past year.
- **Create your annual report.** Start to make copies of your awards. Graph your quarterly results in Excel and print them

out. Then put them in a three-ring binder to be used in your presentation for a raise.

- **Update your LinkedIn profile today.** Use your recent awards or articles you have written to make your profile more interesting to your followers.

CHAPTER 9

Step #6: Create Your Personal ATM

TURN YOUR HOBBY INTO YOUR PERSONAL ATM

You are your own ATM. Not your employer, or your industry . . . *you* are your own Personal ATM. The key is to learn how to tap into it so that it spits out cash whenever you need it, not just when your employer decides it's time to pay. So, how do you get that extra cash to live your Lifestyle by Design?

You turn your hobby into your Personal ATM.

For example, here's what my friend Sandy did. Sandy was a teacher in Southern California. She loved being a teacher and it was part of her Lifestyle by Design. She loved to help kids thrive and reach their potential—it's who she is. Avid fitness buff, tri-athlete, and extreme-sport competitor, she made her life about fulfilling her personal potential, and teaching gave her that outlet. She was so respected that most of her students would come to her to ask for advice and letters of recommendation during their junior and senior years as they began to apply for college. In perfect Sandy fashion, she wanted to do the best possible job and she put her heart and soul into each and every kid she helped, and the results proved it. Her students started to get into the top colleges, and everyone knew that the consultation and road map she provided her students had a lot to do with it. Still, as much as Sandy loved it, her job was taking a toll on her. Because she wanted to deliver so much value at all times and do such a good job, she was working longer hours than the already long hours of a teacher. She was giving many, many late nights and weekends to help her students, but with no extra pay. This was no big deal in the beginning, but once she and her husband had their first child, it all changed. A new baby means having less or no free time.

So, Sandy backed off on the workload because her new obsession was her baby girl. But then something magical happened that doesn't always happen in business: clients—in this case Type A parents—came calling. These were parents who wanted the best for their kids and would stop at nothing to make it happen. They still wanted Sandy's help when it came to their children's college applications and they came calling with cash in their hands.

A lightbulb went off in Sandy's head. She started to see how creating a side business—a side hustle, if you will—could allow her to charge for this assistance, earn extra money, and who knows . . . maybe turn it into something bigger. And as you predicted, that is exactly what happened. Sandy began to charge thousands of dollars for her college admissions counseling services, and within her first year, she realized that this was going to be her full-time career. Her Lifestyle by Design now included her baby, her husband, and her business. She makes four times what she did as a teacher and basically works hard for just three months out of the year, still loving and caring for her baby all the while. Sandy turned her passion for teaching into a hugely profitable Personal ATM, which led to a Lifestyle by Design that fits her perfectly.

When it comes to expanding your earnings, the best thing for you to do is take everything we've talked about when it comes to building your superpower and finding a niche, doing the research and analysis, and looking for the best option to create your own side hustle, your own Personal ATM. It doesn't have to turn into a full-fledged business like Sandy's (but good for you if it does), but if you've maximized your earning potential at your primary job, why not use those late nights and weekends to earn a secondary income and make yourself a millionaire?

PERSISTENCE WINS IN BUSINESS

There's no turning back now. We walked down the road map this far, and now it's go time. You have an idea and you are now going to execute on it to create your own Personal ATM. It might turn into a full-fledged business and a new career for you, or maybe it will just be your side hustle. In either situation, there are certain things that must happen to reduce the odds of failure that plague all new businesses. Fifty percent of all new businesses close in the first year and 90 percent are closed by year five. The odds are tremendously stacked against you and me, if we are like most people. But we are not. My business has stood the test of time—2018 will be our twenty-third year in business. During that time, I have never, *not once*, missed a payroll for an employee, and we pay every Friday. Every single Friday since 1995, I have scraped together enough money to cover every single payroll check that my company has ever issued except one—mine. That's right: On countless weeks, my employees got paid and I didn't. But to me, that was just a temporary setback, a bump in the road, a little hiccup. You will need to have that same outlook as you venture out and build your own Personal ATM. So, let's make sure you learn from me, and together we will build a business that will stand the test of time.

Your mama may have told you that "the most important thing is to just start." That may be true of a lot of things, but when it comes to running a business, the most important thing is to stay in the fight long after the start. The ability to have strong self-esteem, bring value to whatever situation you are in, skill up, do the research and analysis, execute, and then *fight like hell*, and *keep fighting like hell* is how you will make more money.

My company has lasted for twenty-two years, made the *Inc.* magazine Top 500/5000 Fastest-Growing Companies in America for 2014, 2015, 2016, and 2017, as well as the Dallas 100 Fastest-Growing Companies in 2014, 2015, and 2016 because we focus on always executing on the following areas each and every day. You will need to do the same to make it.

COMPANY CULTURE

Just as you've identified and put into place your personal Core Values, you need to do the same when it comes to running a business. Your company culture becomes the core of your Personal ATM, especially when you move it from a hobby to your full-time venture. Company culture is the heartbeat of your Personal ATM. It doesn't matter if you are a one-person shop or you grow it to one thousand people. Your company culture is the single most important thing you will need to get right. Get this right—even if you start with a company of just you, or are keeping it that way—and you will have ease in hiring, firing, managing, growing, and motivating yourself and your staff. If you don't, your Personal ATM will stop spitting out tokens. It will crumble, and I don't want that to happen to you.

The key questions you need to ask and answer yourself when creating your company culture are:

1. **How do you want this business to finish?** Yes, before you start your Personal ATM, you need to see its future. Do you want it to replace your career? Do you want it to eventually go public? Do you want to sell it? Do you want to give it to your kids? Or do you just want it to throw off a few thousand extra bucks a month?

2. What are the Core Values of my business? Much as you did for yourself, now list no more than four Core Values to guide your company. These are the things that you and your team stand for. They will be vital in your long-term success. Here are the four Core Values at my company:

CORE VALUES

Company Profits	Personal Happiness	Customer Loyalty	Preserving Our Reputation
Our creative spirit cannot be enjoyed to the fullest extent without consistent profitability.	We are here because we want to be.	We always recommend the program that benefits our client before benefiting us.	Our business practices are predicated on ensuring our superior reputation within our industry.

3. What do you want the look and feel of the business to be? Literally, down to the paint colors, the uniform colors, the floors, the tile, the chairs, and the computer monitors. Do they represent you? Are you inspired by bold colors, but is your office painted white? Think of it all so that *before* you open the doors and serve the first customer, you have it planned out.

4. What are you willing to tolerate? What type of behavior will you accept from your staff, your clients, and your vendors? Will you offer different compensation plans? Will you allow clients to pay you late? All of it matters. And definitely don't play games with cash or the IRS. Everything is traceable and can eventually come back to bite you. Keep your accounting straight. It will provide you strength and credibility in the marketplace and allow you to sleep a lot better at night.

5. **What are you going to charge your customers?** You already did your research and analysis before you started your Personal ATM and you know there is a market for it. Now set your prices for profitability. How much profit? I will tell you, at a bare minimum, that you need to operate at a 10 percent net profit margin *after* you pay yourself. If you can make more than 10 percent, go for it, but as a starting point, you must earn 10 percent of every dollar you bring in. This means that if you generate $100,000 in sales (revenue), you need to have $10,000 left over *after* you pay yourself. Working your ass off for no profit to show for it at the end of the year will get you nowhere. You must make profits, period.

YOU CAN'T GET A BUSINESS OFF THE GROUND IF NO ONE'S HEARD OF YOU

Nobody knows you. You want to believe that you have some secret sauce that makes what you do valuable to the marketplace, but until you promote it, your potential customers are never going to find you. Promotion can come in various forms, but I can assure you that you will need to do more of it. In my early days of getting CFF off the ground, I took promotion straight to where my customers were: truck stops. I had a sign made that said, *Truck Financing Here.* The sign had two wooden sticks on either side that would slide into the rear doorjambs of my old suburban. I would get up early on Saturday and Sunday mornings and drive to truck stops all over Dallas. I would park, open up the rear doors, put up my sign, and within minutes, truckers would come up to me to talk about financing. It was the simplest and most straightforward form of promotion. When it comes to getting attention, anything goes. You need to use every chance you get to tell people about your Personal ATM. Do the same on your social media pages. They are to be used to promote you, your company brand, and your personal brand. If you've spent time building a personal brand, now is the time to use it to promote your Personal ATM.

FIND WAYS TO OVERDELIVER VALUE

Deliver value greater than your customers' expectations in all situations. Delivering average results won't keep you in the market for long. You might be able to get away with average, middle-of-the-road products and/or services when the economy is good and everyone has money and is willing to spend it, but when the economy turns downward (and it always does), only *exceptional* stays in business. Always give more than your customer expects.

Let's take a real-life example from my personal trainer, Josh.

Josh has worked out with me for almost two years now. He is in great shape and knows his stuff, but like you and me, he needs more money. After many workouts together, he finally asked me for some financial advice. I showed him how he could raise his rates if he found ways to deliver more value to his clients. Josh was charging $50 per session and had fifteen weekly clients who worked out with him an average of three sessions each week. That translates to $2,250 per week, or $9,000 per month. In Josh's case, all he did was work people out. No meal plans, no videos, no body fat index testing, no nutritional or meal prep advice. In short, he offered his clients limited value. He delivered his workouts by showing up prepared each time, but he didn't really *overdeliver*. You can't increase prices without increasing value and overdelivering.

We changed that. I worked with him to create value-added programs and within one week he put all of them into action. Josh signed up for an e-mail marketing program (there are tons, like Constant Contact and MailChimp), loaded in his clients' e-mail addresses, and boom: he had a platform to get value-added messages to them at any time. He created content via a simple one-page weekly e-mail newsletter that went out on Monday mornings at 6:00 a.m. In the newsletter, he offered great recipes for nutritious and easy-to-cook meals. He made nutritional suggestions along with vitamin and supplement recommendations. He told his readers about local farmers' markets in the area and what to buy and eat that was in season. Lastly, he started to record himself doing workouts and embedded them into the newsletter so that his clients could do them on their off days. Get the picture? He started adding a foundation of value-added services that informed, educated, and entertained his client base.

Total time per week? Two additional hours. The result? He was able to raise his rate from $50 per session to $60 per session.

Sure, ten bucks may not seem like much, but he did end up losing a few clients. They didn't see the value-add of the newsletter because they didn't want value, just a cheaper price. I told Josh not to worry. When you add new value, you need to test your client base and the value you bring to them. In Josh's case, he had some cheap clients *and* he was not bringing enough value to them, so they left him. If you raise prices without providing enough value to your clients, some will leave you, too. *And they should!* Value is the key in today's crowded and cloudy marketplace. You must overdeliver value that exceeds the price you charge.

Since Josh lost some clients, he had to get to selling to replace them and find a few more. Only now, he was starting with a new price ($60) and a new product offering. He wasn't just any old trainer; he was now "Josh the Super Trainer," who cared about his clients more than anyone else and proved it each and every week through the content he put in his newsletter. He was now focused on your muscles, your mind, your food intake, and even your relationship. He started asking for referrals from his existing clients and encouraged them to forward his newsletter to their family, friends, and coworkers. I also had him talk to some of the busiest trainers at his gym and ask for their overflow, the clients they were just too busy to take on. Within two weeks, he replaced the clients who dropped out when he raised his prices. It was ridiculously easy to replace them and he actually added three more regulars to his client base, for a total of eighteen.

The end result? Josh now has eighteen very satisfied clients who get his *very* informative weekly newsletter and can watch his specific workouts on their off days. His new clients are all paying $60 per session, for three sessions per week, which equals $12,960 per month, an increase of $3,960 over what he was making before. By overdelivering, and therefore creating more value, he gave himself a nice fat pay raise of $47,520 per year.

UNDERSTAND SCALE

Without question, the biggest regret I have in my business career is that I didn't understand the importance of scale: getting big quickly. When your Personal ATM takes off and starts generating income, you may be tempted to keep it small so that it's comfortable and easy to manage. Big mistake. Buying into BS advice on why staying small was the way to go cost me a decade of my career and millions of dollars. Yes, I said *millions* of dollars. I simply waited too long to get big. When I finally built a business plan to scale my business up to $100 million per year, everything changed for me. I was finally able to make up for all of the years

I stayed too small. If having a big Personal ATM matters to your Lifestyle by Design, it can happen. I'm living proof of it. **If you want to get big, start thinking about how you can best scale up now. Are you going to bring on more people? Become known in your niche? Offer more products or services?**

My entire argument in this book is that you need more money and you need to stay in Accumulation until you get to Rich. So, when your Personal ATM starts to generate the profits, you need to keep the cash. Hoard it. Don't spend it. Don't turn the thermostat down. Don't stop feeding your reserve account.

ACTION STEPS: BUILD YOUR BUSINESS BY DESIGN

- **Write down ideas that you can turn into your Personal ATM.** Be specific and detailed. Leave no stone unturned. Build it out before you start it.
- **Bring value.** Write down three things you do that are valuable. Now write down next to them three things you could do to make them even more valuable. Boom. You now have nine ways to deliver even more value.
- **Core Values, take two.** Just like you did for yourself, write down your Core Values that you want to be part of your business. Put the Doorman in place and don't let anything get in the way of them.

- **Business by design.** Too many people stumble through business just as they stumble through life, going where the current takes them. Write out a detailed plan of what you want your business to look like, and don't turn back until you've made that a reality.

CONCLUSION

Don't Stop Moving the Needle

PICK YOUR NUMBER

I have done the hard math for you. I have offered you tools and strategies that I have used to close my financial gap and make up for lost time. But in order to execute, you will need to do one more thing: Pick your number. **The reason most of us never reach financial success is because we have no idea what our number is, the one we want and need to get us to the end, to the ultimate goal of how much money we want and need over our lifetime, and beyond.** When we make a decision, it requires us to commit and most of us don't want to commit. Why? Because we're scared of failing. It's the same reason we don't like to set goals: because it sucks when we don't meet them. That mindset is disastrous when it comes to money.

How much money do you really want? Is it $1 million? $5 million? $10 million? $100 million? Now that we have covered so much more ground together, I want you to reevaluate, and pick the number that will allow you to live your Lifestyle by Design. Set your sights on getting to that number, commit to throwing all your efforts into getting there, don't look back, and don't slow down until you get there.

Let me go through that again so we all understand. Look at everything you added up in chapter 4 to determine the annual number you need to live the life that you want, and multiply it by the number of years you want to live in that fashion. That's your number. Therefore, if you want to live a Lifestyle by Design that requires $100,000 per year, and you want to live like that for forty years, your number will be $4 million. Don't be scared by that number. Remember, this book is your WAKE-UP CALL and you have to adjust your mind-set to think MUCH BIGGER than you have in the past. You have to think like a Game Facer. If you can expand your mind to believe that you're capable of achieving that number, and focus your grit on getting there, you will get there. The goal is to earn as much as possible for as long as possible. That's how you get into Rich. That's how you maintain your Rich and work toward Wealthy for future generations, so that your kids don't have to start from zero like you and I had to.

You *must* pick your number and build the plan to reach it. That plan to reach it is inside the pages of this book, but here is your recap:

1. Wake up. You don't have enough money, and chances are you're in a state of False Positive.
2. How do you want to live? Design it and find out how much you need to reach it.
3. What is your money gap?
4. Evaluate your money mind-set: are you a Blamer, a Dreamer, or a Game Facer?
5. Are you in Broke, in Accumulation, or in Rich?
6. Can you get to Rich as an employee or do you need to become an employer?
7. Skill up.
8. Earn up.
9. Leverage up.
10. Execute.
11. Pick your number.

The key is to skip the upgrades—today—so you can enjoy the upgrades in the future. Stay true to yourself; only now you know yourself better than you did before this book.

DON'T STOP MOVING THE NEEDLE OF NET WORTH

Reevaluate if you are making enough money for the kind of life you want to live every single year. I reevaluate myself and my progress toward living my Lifestyle by Design every Christmas and ask myself if it's easier to buy presents this year than last year. It helps me think about whether or not I'm moving the needle. You have to create a scoreboard, a barometer, a metrics test that proves to you that you are moving the needle of net worth at levels meaningful enough to get you closer to the finish line. I use Christmas because I can remember purchasing Christmas presents for my boys at the dollar store. And every toy, every sock, every packet of underwear or undershirts made me cringe at the cost. That's why every Christmas is a point of reflection for me. My Christmas reflection is the scoreboard that I now use to determine if I made more money than I did last year. Of course, you can use your budget, your bank statements, your personal financial statement, or whatever math you want to use. But I know deep down, even after I've done all that stuff and the math tells me that I'm far better off this Christmas than I was last year, that if I'm not emotionally more confident in my purchasing power this year than I was last year, then I'm not moving the needle of my net worth. **Every quarter, I suggest you take out your personal financial statement and redo it. This will help you stay focused on moving the needle of net worth often.**

We are close to the end now and we have covered so much ground. I'm so proud of you for getting this far and I hope two things:

1. **This information has been helpful.** That would mean so much to me. To know that the process that I have taken to

secure the financial future of myself, my family, my employees, my clients, and my vendors was helpful to you. I'm also
hopeful that it won't take you as long as it took me. You can
do it faster if you use these strategies. You can beat me, and I
want you to.

2. **You are special.** I know I yelled at you a lot, but it's only because I knew you could take it. You would have never read
this far if you were not ready to go to the next level, and the
next level is attainable for you. You are now in Game Facer
territory. Whatever the chains of your upbringing, the advice
you got or didn't get, they're all broken. Now let's get you rich.
Scaling way up matters more than ever. Keep dreaming big,
keep going for more and more revenue.

ALL OF IT MATTERS

My brother-in-law John's story is the reason for this book. Bad
things happen to good people, and John was one of the good
ones. But more than anything, John's story made me realize two
things. First, those bad things—whether they affect your health,
career, or living situation—don't affect just you, they impact everyone around you. Second, a lot of those repercussions, such as
emotional pain, worries about the future, or just a temporary hit
to your ego, are solved by having more money. It may seem obvious that money helps solve problems, but as I travel and speak to
people, I'm constantly amazed by how few of us do anything to
improve our money situation. If you take nothing more from this

book, please take that concept with you. Money matters and I, you, we need more of it.

You made it through, so I want to thank you and share how the story of my brother-in-law, John, concluded.

I was conducting our standard morning scrum meeting at CFF when my phone started to ring. It was Rokki, and I didn't answer because we were in the meeting. But when Rokki wants to be heard, she makes sure she gets heard, so she kept calling. I picked up on the third call and she told me what I feared was coming. John had just passed and she was on her way to the hospital. I told my team to carry on without me, and dropped everything to get to the hospital, too. Almost one year to the day after our families got the grim news of John's cancer diagnosis, we got the worst news any family ever wants to hear. John died at 9:22 a.m.

If you haven't been with a person and their family minutes after their death, you can't go there with me; but if you have, you know what I saw and heard. John's wife, Lori, was screaming as his only son, John, crawled into the hospital bed with his father and refused to let go. His daughter Hannah was inconsolable, and so was my Rokki. My mother-in-law, Gigi, was gray and motionless. Every single nurse on that floor, and even some who were not working at that time, raced in to give their condolences. He had won them over, too. They cried just like we did because after seeing so much pain on that cancer floor over the years, they knew that this patient, my brother-in-law, Rokki's brother, Gigi's only son, Lori's high school sweetheart and husband, and

Hannah's, John's, Zoey's, and Lizzie's father, John Bryan Eibert, was special. Amid our grief, John looked peaceful. His fight was over and he was ready to meet his keeper. But the rest of us were not ready to let him go. John died sooner than we expected. Just two weeks before, the doctors had blasted him with a massive chemo cocktail in a last-ditch effort to kill the cancer. We all knew it was going to be a massive dose, and the doctors said if it didn't work, he would have three to six months to live. But pneumonia set in and so did a virus in his bloodstream, and he was gone within two weeks.

John's funeral went just the way he would have wanted it. Plenty of Guns N' Roses played in the background as pictures of his life played on the big screen. People came from everywhere. It was a little like the ending of the movie *Big Fish:* people who were just characters in the stories he told us all appeared.

My Rokki says she sees him often in her dreams. It makes her so happy when she dreams about him. She says he has a glow about him and there is always a bird with him. We all still feel his presence in our lives. On numerous occasions, we have had a single bird appear inside our house. We have no idea how it gets in. No door or window is open, yet we find a bird inside our house, sitting calmly on a piece of furniture until we open the door and let it out. Sometimes Rokki won't open the door for a while, so she can take in as much of the moment as she can. She knows it's John checking on her and it makes her happy. I have flown countless miles on airplanes, and for all of the airports I have been in, I have never seen a bird inside an airport terminal;

but on two separate occasions when I was traveling with Rokki after John died, a bird has come up and perched itself on a chair close to her. Try to tell Rokki that the bird is not John? She will kick your ass and I will be right there with her.

You now know how it happened. How John's story of being a wonderful son, brother, father, and husband made the lives of everyone around him better. You also know what happens when you don't pay attention—close attention—to your money situation, regardless of how sweet and kind you are; it can cause pain and suffering for those around you long after you are gone.

We don't usually have what we think we have, especially when it comes to time. When it comes to our health, our finances, or our careers, we put off fixing our problems, because we think we have the time to "make it up." And then, one day, you get the news that your time is up. Prepare early.

Money is emotionless. Money doesn't care that you are nice and loving and caring. Money is its own animal. It makes no guarantees or promises. It responds when you give it attention and can bite you in the ass when you don't. If you don't make money, understand it, skill up to earn it, save it, do research and analysis to invest and protect it, it will not be there for you. But when you put all the tools, tips, and strategies in this book into action, and approach money with clarity and focus and effort, you will realize that it is just a cog in the wheel of your life. Once you master it, money becomes submissive and rolls over for you to dominate it.

STICK TO THE ROAD MAP

Congratulations—you've made it to the end of this book and are well on your way to having more money. Just stick to the road map, which will take you to where you want to go. If you want to get rich, you have to be tough. Set big, unattainable goals, and then blow past them as you achieve more than you dreamed you were capable of. You deserve this. You are worthy. You have the skills. You can build your Lifestyle by Design. You can make up the gap created by your old ways. You're ready. You are a Game Facer. Drop me a note and keep me informed of your progress. We are together in your journey. Nothing would make me happier than to hear your story of how your success turned you into a fellow Game Facer and that you've blown past me. The ball is in your court. It always has been; you just needed a little motivation and guidance. I hope that you take everything we have covered in this book and use it to reach each and every goal and dream you and your family deserve.

#staygritty

—Matt

ACKNOWLEDGMENTS

The pleasure of working with professionals in their industry is never ending. During the creation and writing of this book, I have had the pleasure of working with some of the best. It is with deep gratitude that I thank the following people:

I am grateful to my coworkers at Commercial Fleet Financing, Inc. Over the years you have believed in me and the vision of CFF. But vision got us only so far. We put in the massive amount of work required, and together we built a great company that has stood the test of time.

Thank you, Steve Carlis and Hank Norman of 2 Market Media in New York City. Both of you helped me learn to be me.

Thank you to Arestia Rosenberg. You write like I think.

Thank you to my agent, Nena Madonia Oshman of Dupree Miller & Associates in Dallas. You showed me the ropes.

ACKNOWLEDGMENTS

Thank you to my editor, Kaushik Viswanath, at Portfolio Penguin. We make a good team.

I never miss a chance to say thank you to my wife, Rokki, and our three boys, John, Jack, and Julian. You all gave me the time to tell Uncle John's story in a way that can help thousands of people for years to come.

John Eibert, RIP.

INDEX

INDEX